ANCHOR BOOKS

EXPRESSIONS FOR A NEW CENTURY FROM THE SOUTH WEST

Edited by

Kelly Deacon

First published in Great Britain in 2000 by
ANCHOR BOOKS
Remus House,
Coltsfoot Drive,
Woodston,
Peterborough, PE2 9JX
Telephone (01733) 898102

HB ISBN 1 85930 774 4
SB ISBN 1 85930 779 5

Foreword

Anchor Books is a small press, established in 1992, with the aim of promoting readable poetry to as wide an audience as possible. We see ourselves as a platform for new and established poets to built upon their talents and see their work in print for possibly the first time.

Each of the chosen poems has been specifically favoured from a large selection of entries sent. As always the editing proved to be a difficult task and as the edition, the final selection was mine.

Expressions For A New Century From The South West is a unique collection of poetry and verse written in a variety of styles and themes, brought to us from many of today's modern and traditional writers, who reside in this area. The poems are easy to relate to and encouraging to read, offering engaging entertainment to their reader.

This delightful collection is sure to win your heart, making it a companion for life and perhaps even earning that favourite little spot upon your bookshelf.

Kelly Deacon
Editor

Contents

Catching Francesca

My granddaughter climbed upon a chair,
with laughing eyes and shining hair.
She looked at me
and seemed to say,
'I'm going to jump - I dare.'

She held her arms up high.
She jumped.
It must have seemed to her
as if she was reaching for the sky.
- I caught her.

She continued this game
for quite some time - of fear, no trace!
Flinging her arms wide,
flying through space!
Each time - I caught her.

She is still so tiny
and has trust in us all.
She knew I would catch her
and not let her fall.
And - I caught her.

I hope as she grows
she will keep that trust.
That life will not fail her
and turn her dreams into dust.
I hope there will always be someone around,
to catch her - before she falls to the ground.

Patricia Nelson

Love

I drift through you,
Like a ship through the sea,
Such peace I never knew,
Such peace you give to me.

You are to me as I am to myself,
I perceive through your eyes,
To others' entreaties, I am deaf,
This happiness can't be lies.

You're my oxygen mask,
Filtering out life's waste,
Life isn't an easy task,
I've caused pain in my haste.

Too easy to become cynical,
To say there is no true happiness,
But that would be hypocritical
And make our love pointless.

Fantasy replaces reality,
I think I love, therefore I do,
Maybe I've lost my sanity,
To feel this way about you.

This insanity I welcome,
Into your words I sink,
You speak and I feel at home,
I am, I don't have to think.

Daniel Sloman

THE FORTRESS

Still the cows calmly graze
On green hillsides.
The few surviving
Buttercups yield to the same
Wind's hands and in a silver stream
Below the wood, swim the fish:
Part of the dream.

But across the heath bulldozers bring
Yet another motorway
And the sickly spread of the town.
So I will build a fortress
From the pieces that remain -
Birds' song, flowering hedges
And the besieged village field
Where cricket once was played.

I'll make a magic circle with my skein
Of memories by the tadpole pond
And built a mental cage against
The business parks.

Knowing that the moon will shine on
Corporate man, motor-car and pylon
With the disregard
It once reserved for lovers
In the hay lofts and foxes
In the bracken.

Tim Williams

Forbidden Love

My mind reaches out to hold you
Yet my arms stay by my side
As you turn and walk away from me
A small part of me dies
I try to look in deeper
Far beneath those gorgeous eyes
To see if there's mutuality
As my burning heart's denied
I scream out to the inertia
That's tearing out my heart
At least when I close my eyes
We are no longer apart
I feel your breath against my lips
As your fingers stroke my face
But then I open my eyes again
And find you've still walked away

Karen Churchward

The Wrong Planet

I am on the wrong planet
I step out onto alien territory
Beware the false grin, the elusive smile
I see straight through your glossy front
Beneath the make-up and false perm
Who is there?
We march, keeping the layers well protected
If you show me yours, I might show you mine
Better to stay concealed beneath a cold front
A frosty smile, an icy stare,
I must not crack, or shatter my illusion
That I exist, out there.

Nicola Belle

Ebony Man

He'll ride the waves towards me,
Come running up the land,
He'll take me in his arms
And gently kiss my hand.

Far from his native country,
Apart from his native race,
Living in a land so strange,
This will be our place.

Concrete replaces grass,
Metal fills the trees,
People swarm around,
Anonymous honeybees.

Onto the boat we climb,
And slowly join the stream,
Sailing away from ignorance,
We begin to live our dream.

Lives together, intertwined,
Joined through and through,
Passionate romantic nights,
The stream a deep dark blue.

The waves begin to grow now,
Smashing on the shore,
Dreams torn up and lost now,
Lost for evermore.

If we'd sailed a different course,
Swam another stream,
Taken a different direction,
What would all this mean?

Would the stream be blue,
Or still be red with blood?

Philippa Larcombe

THE ANGRY WASP

The angry wasp I cannot trust,
His way are unpredictable
I'd say avoidance is a must,
He'll find your nose delectable!
Or land upon your chin or arm,
To spear you with his lance
Then leave you screaming in alarm
And buzz off while you dance.
'Don't be afraid,' your dad will say
And swipe it with his paper,
Then very likely run away,
To reappear much later.
There's no good reason for this spite,
He simply loves that spearful,
So waits until you're sitting tight
And feeling pretty cheerful.
He aims to change the mood around
And leave somebody tearful.
God's creatures go about the world
To their appointed lot,
It seems to me the wasp was hurled
At our most tender spot.

Ann Elliott Wall

POETRY

Poetry is the temple of the soul,
a dwelling place upon the threshold
of ancient night, bathed in
the luminous presence of an ancestral moon;
that amplifier of oceans,
and of heightened states of awareness.

Within this sacred space,
drawn by inner certainty
and the prophetic call of an ageless mystery,
the initiate in us is blessed to receive
the sacrament of love,
ever renewing and ever reborn.

Alan Davies

A DAY LATER

I messed up this time -
Your only crime
Was to extend a tender hand
Which I bit,
Yesterday I could smile
Tomorrow I'll spend in denial
Today the truth just hurts
I've done wrong
And now you're gone.

The sun cuts my skin to the bone
What's the point in being illuminated
When you're all alone?

I made a mistake -
You want a break
And I just thought you wanted out
Now you're gone.
Yesterday I could live
Tomorrow I'll wish you could forgive
Today the truth just hurts
I've done wrong
And now you're gone.

Damon Naile

HOMAGE TO THE HILLS

When there's no friend to share your days
Head to the heights to cure all ills,
Many times have trodden these ways,
Ardour undimmed on Malvern Hills.

Once on the hills compelled higher,
Past St Anne's Well, path wide and long,
Gushing stream tinkling like a lyre
In harmony with the bird-song.

Sitting beneath my favourite pine,
Lost awhile in deep devotion,
Here where I worship all is fine,
While heart is filled with emotion.

Looking south along ancient track
Stretching as far as eye can see,
In the wilderness nothing lack,
This where our creator must be.

Turning to survey the Severn Plain
Feel the wind gently caressing,
Surrounded by hills, sun or rain,
Homage to the landscape blessing.

Drawn to the vision that is mine,
Drank from the well of happiness,
All below splendid in sunshine,
Buildings of Malvern blend no less.

Filled with nostalgia for life past
That still catches one by the throat,
Hope remains to the very last,
Contentment reigns on hills remote.

Betty Mealand

My Fairy Prince

I loved you so, my fairy prince,
I loved you as no other since.
Handsome, dark and debonair,
Tall and strong, without a care
You came and so ensnared my heart
I thought that we would never part.
We met and walked in secret places
Lay where moss the earth embraces;
We sat and talked, exchanged a kiss
And felt that life was total bliss.
We stood beside the gentle stream
And watched the silver fishes gleam,
We stood beneath the starry skies
And saw the crescent moon arise
To give a tiny friendly light
To cast away the fears of night.
We laughed and played upon the grass
And watched the dancing shadows pass.
We did not plan for future years,
Talked not of distant hopes and fears.
We took our pleasures as they came
And thought 'twould always be the same.
I loved you so I could not bear
To think of life without you there.
I never shall forget the day
When first I heard you'd gone away,
I thought that I should surely die,
We hadn't even said goodbye.
We'd sat upon a five barred gate
For you were ten and I was eight.

M Hall

UNIVERSE

On one hand they shoot for the stars, for the future.
They are looking at pinpricks in space.

On the other they delve inside, into matter.
They are seeking to protect their place.

In between and almost unnoticed, unwanted
On a thin red line
Marching to a frenetic time
Balancing between the two infinities
Are . . . us.

We too have our extremes and extremities.
We are pulled by forces in all directions.
We are pushed and squeezed by time.

We rattle in a cage of hours,
Held inside a chamber of weeks
In a fortress of years.

As we progress, the targets change
There is a spiral leading away from established themes
There are daily chores that we dismiss, we ignore.
There is not time.

As we are aiming towards new universes
We are diving into uncertainty
The rush excites and blinds.

Tall towers stand as tombstones
Testaments to a tomorrow that comes and goes
Automobiles now fight our animal battles and belch
Their secret dragon breath.
We sit protected in their lacquered cocoons,
Quadraphonic and fuel injected.

We still act on impulse, electrical impulse.
Red light, green light,
Phosphorous glow and enzyme bright.

The litany of our desires
Drop like grains of sand through
The hour glass . . . enumerated.
Car, house, wage, career
Eventually, even these exceed grammar,
TV, CD, VCR.

Meanwhile, from the mists of our horizons
Twin cohorts of the apocalypse gallop,
From the micro and the macro, to swallow all.

S N W Cross

Pity-Me And Woe-Is-Me

Pity-Me and *Woe-is-Me* were walking hand in hand
Labouring each other with spoken thoughts they solely understand;
Attentive to self-interest without regard for others,
Their self-affection for their woes make them kindred brothers.

Lamenting their discomfort and lack of worldly goods,
With self-consuming envy deploring others' livelihoods;
Wracked with deep self-pity and bemoaning their position,
They only have themselves to blame to be in their condition.

Self-centre and self-interest seem to be their faction,
Subjected to the contemplation of their own self-action.
If they could cast themselves in the position of their shadow,
What would the view be of themselves and what future they foreshadow?

Bryan Colman Bird

GRANNY'S STORY

Granny did such things in the war
Had never been heard of before.
Bombs screaming down and aircraft flack
Found her lying flat on her back
In a shelter deep underground
The Air Raid Warden coming round.
He was a nice man, took a peek
At Granny lying fast asleep.
The sky lit up with lurid glow
Dead or alive? How could he know?
He pulled her legs she gave a yell
And said 'I don't feel very well.'

He went away, rescued a child,
Houses fell down no one smiled.
He used his shaded torch to see
Where he could help this misery.
A bomb came down, he hit the ground
As earth exploded all around.
He wished he had a cup of tea
And cursed the German enemy.
Old folk remember, young don't know
How evil festered long ago.
Granny got up, hobbled away
And lived to tell this tale today.

The Air Raid Warden with a drum
Welcomed the new millennium.

Ruth Mollon

Ode To A Daughter-In-Law

I truly love my daughter-in-law,
she's really very kind,
I just wish she was not so clever
had such an agile mind.

Baby buggies and umbrellas
take on a life of their own
I always lose the ticket
jam up the parking zone.
I do

I get up in the morning determined to take care,
she is standing with a leaking milk carton
'We always know when Grannie's here'
she says.

Why is it when we are going out
and I take ages to get dressed
she has to twitch my hair
pull my collar showing vest
she does.

Why is it when I make a cake I spill all the sugar
forget to put the eggs in and make my grandsons snigger.
They do.

They are all so kind to me and care for me I'll own
But it is truly marvellous when I walk into my home.

Joan Boss

MARCH

Crocuses poke their bright heads through the grass,
Yellow and blue gems on a green canvas.
Barren and silent are standing the trees,
Their buds swelling to break into the spring.

Something has changed imperceptibly and
The afternoon dusk is about to end.
At five o'clock the sun still wanders high
And bird-song wakes at dawn the chilly sky.

Wild winds of spring are waking nature up,
They blow recklessly, stirring up the sap
In dormant cells, that will burst into life
To greet joyously the oncoming March.

Soft, lukewarm rains now incessantly spray
Left patches of snow, that slowly melt away
On muddy fields and bring out all the green
In a tender and translucent sheen.

As I am walking just across the park,
Something quietly grips my tired heart:
Shall I see new spring calling me next year,
Or shall tracelessly from earth disappear?

Arpad Sarmezey

MODERN AMERICAN DISEASE

The shortest, quickest poem; the cheapest, biggest rhyme,
Announcing and recording the American decline.
Where continual pursuits of eat, shop, drink and drive,
Dictate, discard and move on, in order to survive.
The unnecessary food left, rotting on a plate,
The same systematic process of urban fabric fate.

The cracks and leaks and fissures; the tracts of land laid waste
Like the vile and rotting stomach in a body of distaste.
I can't believe you'll stop it,
This American decline
By applying a perfumed bandage
To a cancer of the spine.

Marian Cross

A Winter's Tale

This is a winter's tale,
Of wind and rain and gale.
Snow and ice, not very nice,
Children looking pale.

Then suddenly they come to life,
A snowball fight begins.
Shouts and laughing fill the air,
No one cares who wins.

Rolling the snow into a ball,
A snowman has begun.
First a large, then a small,
It's such a lot of fun.

Hat and scarf, pipe and eyes,
He looks a proper guy.
Then the sun comes, shining bright
And it's goodbye snowman, bye-bye.

Now the winter's over,
Spring is on the way.
Daffodils are coming out,
Hooray I say hooray.

Winifred Shore

SWEAT

Feel the dangerous heat,
as moisture rolls and meets.

Collecting on the brow,
seeking a furrow.

From the swell it spills,
to the gully betwixt the hills.

Down a rivulet ran,
weaving through the tan.

Unaware it curves,
over pores and grooves.

Down glistening skin,
to the valley of sin.

Colin Gardner

BEN

I wish I was an animal,
Like my dog all day.
He walks, eats and plays away.
He never works or goes to school,
He'd much rather jump in a pool and play the fool.
He never talks but knows the time.
He likes the mud and cosy chairs.
He wags his tail to tell a tale.
He walks about so very proud, as if he owns the place,
and sometimes sneaks to get his way.
He guards fearlessly and hates all cats.
He barks at odd men and chases the vicar's fat pet.
He's quite a hound we have found to share our busy days.

Rita Jane Williams

I Was Saved

Jesus you saved me
This I know,
I had an empty soul
Drifting where the wind would blow,
Then I heard you say
Child stay a while
And I did
And you have made my life worthwhile
You have picked me up when I fell
Helped me over many a stile.
Thank you Lord for saving me
You are so kind and sweet,
I know you love and cradle me
Even when I sleep.

Shirley Rowland

Tapestry Of Love

I'll weave a heart of love for you
with golden silks, and ribbons blue,
I'll fill it with a love so dear -
to last you through the coming years,
I'll embroider in the centre space -
with lovers' knots, and Belgium lace,
Then along the pique edge I'll sew -
pearl droplets, like a bubble-glow.
Then within this 'Heart of Dreams'
I'll tuck a ruby in a seam,
To mark the place where our love will grow -
and bloom with age forever.

P I Bradford

AUTUMN

I hate autumn because it's wet and muddy underfoot,
The dog takes such an age to clean and dry.
I hate autumn when the wind strips the leaves from the trees
And scatters them all in such a mess.
I hate autumn with all those spiders' webs hung with dew
There's always one right across your path.
I hate autumn when the flowers die and the garden looks so sad,
The battle with the pests is over but the lawn still needs a trim.
I hate autumn because of Hallowe'en
All those children greedy for their treats.
I hate autumn because of bonfire night,
The smell and the noise that frightens our pets
And all that money up in smoke!
I hate autumn as the days get shorter
And you don't know how to dress.
But most of all I hate autumn when overnight there's been a frost
And the stiffened leaves now shimmer in the early morning light.
Shhh . . .
Close your eyes and breathe in deep,
You could almost believe in magic!

Elizabeth Whiting

THE BROWN SAND DUNES OF BERROW

It was summer and the days were long and balmy,
And the sand stretched to the sea so far away
As we lay upon the brown sand dunes of Berrow
On the first day of that special holiday.

In the distance a container ship was passing
On its way from Avonmouth to who knows where,
But for us upon the brown sand dunes of Berrow
The world could pass and never leave a care.

We knew this joy just couldn't last for ever,
The time would come when we would have to go
And take leave of the brown sand dunes of Berrow
And the places all around we'd come to know.

'Tis our last day on the brown sand dunes of Berrow,
A place that we have come to hold so dear,
But no matter where the world around us beckons
Be sure that we'll return again next year.

Geoff Tullett

The Dream

I saw the storm clouds gather
The lightning called my name
You though were not beside me
My world can never be the same
The trees were still, leaves golden
A bird sang so sweetly overhead
As raindrops fell like music
Your words were running through my head
I walked across the meadow
Passed the stream so clear and bright
Remembering all those lovely days
And many, many precious nights
Within my hand I held a crystal
Rose pink for a love warm and true
You gave me that so long ago
Saying, I love only you
A kiss was felt upon my face
From lips soft as morning dew
It was just a restless unhappy dream
I awoke and still had you.

Elizabeth Cowley-Guscott

A SUMMER'S DAWN

What a wonderful glittering glow of
the dawn,
A beauty to be captured on paper as
a new day has been born,
The bright shimmering film from the
distant sun,
Breaking through that slight mist on
its daily run,
Making another warm clear day without
any rain,
A beautiful picture to be observed
from the windowpane,
As you listen to the cooing of the
doves, from the green meadow,
Trying to keep in tune with the sun rays
all aglow,
Such beauty can be seen all around at that
break of day,
Like soft warm hands reaching out to
touch, as they say,
But at first an unbelievable, uncanny silence
all around,
Suddenly, a far distant travelling railway
engine did sound,
Which seem to mingle with the calls
of magpies and crows,
But, nothing appeared to disturb the
dawn beauty, as it grows,
Into a breathtaking array of colours
as if from another world,
Of reds, whites, blues, even the clouds
like flags, seem to unfurl,
Thinly stretched across that blue
large open sky,
What colours, what beauty could be seen
up there so high,

Whilst slowly that scarlet cloak unfolds
so much more,
Bathing the world it seems in warmth as
on upwards it soars.

John S Johns

GOODBYE GOD WWW.

Where once stood God's finest creation,
now stands the empty shell of man,
unshackled from all forms of guilt,
he grasps his pleasures where he can,
for now there is only degradation left,
for sexes became the same,
having learnt to mutilate all creation,
we hurtle back to from where we came.

Perhaps it's as in the book,
but who has the time to read,
we spent years proving God was wrong,
so for his religion we have no need,
computers and the Internet,
that's how the new world stacked,
and any nation that has a god,
well they're just holding their people back,

Sadly I think we may be wrong,
for I peeked at a couple of pages,
the last chapter in the book,
reflects well our modern ages,
so you carry on my friend,
I am sure you're doing well,
I just want to read some more,
for I think we've just found hell.

Simon Woollen

The Missing Attribute

Once we were proud to be English,
We took pride in what we had done,
We were cheered for our inventions
And praised for the prizes won.

The police and law were respected,
The church was firm and true,
The sick and old were cared for;
Which was no more than their due.

Now streets are littered and dirty,
Our shops are plagued by crime;
The trains and buses could do with a wash
And seldom run on time.

With the law no longer reliable
And the church no longer sure,
Crimes no longer punished -
There's no justice any more.

People wearing patched up jeans,
Like workmen's bib and brace,
With studs in tongue and stomachs,
Ears, nose and every place!

They have money to spend on luxuries
And plenty for trips abroad,
They have time to waste on leisure,
Far more than they can afford.

They have all that life can offer,
More than they should expect.
But what they need and haven't got,
They haven't got *self respect.*

G C Kay

The Mission

Sent by the Air Force on a mission to Colerne
I landed near a city.
I very soon realised it was Bath
For the girls there were oh so pretty!

Having always found dancing to be a pleasure
I targeted the pavilion.
There I found a partner supreme
She really was 'one in a million'.

The Air Force had given me thrills galore,
For which I can never atone
But I'd never flown so high in my life,
As on the day when I met Joan.

The war continued and I was sent
To places far away.
Yet life in the Air Force became more of a joy,
For Joan wrote me a letter each day.

Air Force discomforts were put in the shade
As I continued to travel the lands.
Joan was my permanent partner
And my future was in very safe hands.

Eventually I was demobilised,
I'd been navigated to peace.
Joan was my real live compass,
Whose guidance will never cease.

Our wedding took place at Weston All Saints,
The build up you've heard me relate,
But I owe more than I've shown
To the Air Force and Joan
For what happened in May, '48.

C A Brush

Nam

Sacrosanct in his panzer tank
He strolls along the highway
With his hippie dreams
And a great big gun
A flash of light instant inspiration
And when the sparks are gone
He keeps wandering on
Till the times he remembers they are gone

Sanctified and consecrated
Sacred ways to pass on down the highway
And when he dreams the nightmare lingers on
The smell of napalm is so strong early in the morning
He reaches for the crumpled cigarette packet
Confusion reigns as he finds his hand is gone
A bloody stump for a trigger finger
Solemn moments as his mind recalls

Thunderous sound and his mind it was shattered
A moment's respite as his eyes flick open wide
Shivering in the pool of sweat that he lies in
The smell of napalm lingers in the bedroom
Or is it sex that smells so strong
Spinning head from so many empty bottles
Itchy dick and empty wallet
Laughter next door it sounds so loud

Splash of water cold and refreshing
Bleary eyes unfocussed empty and cold
Unsure who it is that they are looking upon
Dead eyes staring back from the mirror
Cruel face that is set in stone
Another day another itchy trigger finger
Down the highway out of Saigon
On a mission with a great big gun.

John D Vennard

Of Royal Blood

It was in the first century AD
That Joseph of Arimathea arrived,
He left Judea after the crucifixion
Making sure Jesus had survived.

Joseph was forced to leave Judea
Because of unrest and suspicions,
He had taken his hereditary name
And left with his Nazarene companions.

Joseph's message was the true word
Whilst Paul made Jesus mythical,
Making a god out of a man
Which left us devoutly critical.

He arrived at the shores of Britain
With his group of followers the story goes,
Landing at what is now Glastonbury
Once an island so long ago.

Joseph brought with him the Holy Grail
Not a cup which legends relate,
But a royal bloodline of David
Brought in bodily state.

Within his body ran royal blood
Of a kingly line he descended,
For Joseph was James, the brother of Jesus
The bloodline of which has never ended.

From Jesus and James through royal houses
The Grail line is preserved,
To be continued with the throne secure
And the Holy Grail of David's line preserved.

David G Forsbrook

CARDBOARD CITY

Cardboard city they call it, 'tis my humble abode,
Where the pavement for the night is my bed,
Awoken by the cold on my fingers,
Still 'tis better than waking up dead,

I lie looking up to the stars in the sky,
Feel the frost creeping into my bones
And the fellow beside me is snoring,
I prod him, he lets out a moan,

My possessions, I carry them with me,
Stuffed into a white plastic bag,
There is nothing of value inside it,
'Cept a photo of me and me dad,

I'm not here for the drugs or the drinking,
Perhaps it's fate brings me here to this place,
For the cards that were dealt through my lifetime,
Not one was the card called an ace.

Here I sit with my coat pulled around me,
And my hat pulled down over my face,
Seventeen is my life really over,
Am I cast to one side from this race,

As I gaze at the photo before me,
The picture now faded and torn,
There are times in my life when I'm wishing,
Yes I'm wishing, I'd never been born.

John W Bendle

A Time

A time to live and a time to die,
A time to be happy, a time to cry,
A time to seek peace, a time to seek war,
A time to be rich, a time to be poor.

A time for love, a time for hate,
A time to get on, a time to wait,
A time for good and a time for bad,
A time to be sane, a time to be mad.

A time to be cruel, a time to be kind,
A time to lose, a time to find,
A time to climb, a time to fall,
A time to shrink, a time to grow tall.

A time for yourself, a time for others,
A time for enemies, a time for lovers,
A time for youth, a time for age,
A time for calmness, a time for rage.

A time to be caged, a time to be free,
A time to be blind, a time to see,
A time to remember, a time to forget,
A time that was happy, a time to regret.

A time unfeeling, a time to care,
A time to be selfish, a time to share,
A time to blame, and a time to forgive,
A time to die and a time to live.

There will always be a time.

Julie Belinda White

Do They Care?

I'm invisible,
They walk past and wave their noses in the air,
I starve and freeze, shivering to death.
But do they care?

Every day, the same old story,
Excuse me, could you spare some change, please,
They leave me, sitting on the stone cold floor.
But do they care?

Sometimes, they stop and stare at me,
I build up my hopes, look up and smile,
They walk on by, heads hung low.
But do they care?

Dogs will come up to me,
Sniff my damp, smelly bed and bark,
Hold their legs up in the air, yuk.
But do they care?

Occasionally they come up to me,
Give me a fiver, a cup of tea,
I smile and feel wanted again.
They really do care!

Natalie Hudson (13)

Ever An Optimist!

'Why do you want to watch rugby?' I said.
'It's those muscly men with hairy legs!'
So I watched, and was hooked.
Number fifteen is a gorgeous bloke,
Tall and athletic. So perfect he looked.

I've spoken with him many a time
And I know he's already taken
But it must be said girlfriends
Come and go . . .
Unless I am mistaken.

Rebecca Waters (17)

MINDBLOWN

Mindblown,
Staring out my head.
Mindblown,
Brain is numb and touch unfed.

Sitting in my vacuum,
Eclipse the world in one small room.
Sounds are fleeting, distant roar,
Disconnected to my core.

Flashes of my life gone by,
Red and hot my body cries.
Sensing that I'm all alone,
Mind a child, but body grown.

Notions of a love gone by,
Life remote I slowly die.
Drowning in a wave of grief,
Emptiness beyond belief.

Mindblown,
Staring out my head.
Mindblown,
Brain is numb and touch unfed.

Julia Bowler

Pie In The Sky

On holiday in Somerset,
The weather was just grand.
Fancied a snooze upon the beach.
Spread my towel out on the sand.
Was there peace and tranquillity
in that secluded bay?
No, the squalling, squabbling seagulls
kept me wide awake all day.

Next day began with drizzle,
but by noon the sun was bright.
Bought myself some fish and chips,
mouth watering with delight.
Sat upon the seafront wall
to eat my tasty dish.
Down swooped a raiding seagull
which stole my blasted fish.

Last day, I met a gorgeous girl.
We strolled across the moors.
'Give me a kiss for luck,' she said,
'before we go indoors.'
So I took off my sunhat.
Who said romance was dead?
Sweet lips met mine, then, suddenly,
A gull *sh*t* on my head.

I'm visiting the same hotel
next year, perhaps July.
I hope that on their menu
will be Somerset Seagull Pie.

J Bates

You Say You Know Me!

Who am I - you say you know,
This path I can assure is slow.

Perhaps impossible my reply, my needs and actions may not clarify,
Who you think am I.

My thumb print, eyes and features, only fragments of the self,
Some telltale signs of wear and tear and worries on the shelf.

My mouth may utter gibberish faint at times,
Renderings of surface mind, a sea of turmoil's myths and rimes.

And yet you see - I may give hint of me.

Within my frame, a tale of who am I,
A genetic code, a cell, a nuclei.

I am a mist, a spirit calm, a storm, the sunlight on your arm,
I am life, and mean no harm, lest spite you show that changeth calm.

I am the Devil and Godchild of your dreams, and all that you perceive,
Take care - who wish to know me, lest self will be revealed.

Who am I

In resolve this quest to languish rest,
To love one's self not others test.

In my demise I seek to see, a world eternal you and me,
Not who am I, nor who are they, but peace and calm - and as I lay,
That all around me is as one, and self with me is harmony.

I am the night, I am the day, I am life at play

I am you.

Barry Graham-Dowthwaite

A Promise

If you await in robe of white,
Patient, in paradise my love,
More glorious than the stars above
Or lilies bathed in heavenly light;
Then I shall take your slender hand
And straight, before the Godhead stand

And ask Him thus: (We side-by-side
Restored for all eternity)
'How could You take my love from me?
For sweeter person never died
When in full, radiant joy of youth:
Unbowing, I demand the truth!'

Though aeons pass till He reply
I wait, your gentle hand in mine,
Then if He say 'twere act divine'
(And you too pure for such as I)
Then should I reverence display
For He who took my world away?

Or He declare 'For merest earth
She was too beauteous to behold:
I saw a perfect bloom unfold
And truly judged its greater worth.'
Then, still unbowing, I must know
Why He, all-powerful, made you so.

But might He say 'You worshipped her,
Revering her as one divine
And loved her more than Me, yet Mine
The throne where Godly men defer:
Your adoration for this maid
It seemed a pagan soul displayed'

Then I shall bend as sinner ought,
Confessing it was truly so;
Acknowledging that God must know
Our every deed, each secret thought,
That God is wise, all things above:
Yet kneeling at *your* feet my love.

Paul de Mapingham

No Time This Time

'It's great to see you,
I haven't seen you since . . .
has it been that long?
How's . . . and the kids?
Can't stop,
I'm in a rush,
I've got so much to do,
there's never enough time,
is that the time?
How time flies,
I should have been at . . .
ages ago.
We must meet up again,
keep in touch,
I promise we'll . . .
maybe next week?
Call me,
I'll phone you,
it's been good to see you,
give my love to . . .
take care,
cheers for now,
must dash,
taxi!'

Jon Perigud

Homeless

The village garage has closed down
The pumps are dry, the forecourt bare,
The office gone - repair bays too,
Mechanics no longer whistle there.
Then, vandalised - all windows smashed
The garage doggedly stood there.
Each spring, although an empty shell
It was home . . . to a special pair.
The garage had a welcome beam
On which to place their cup shaped nest.
They swooped in through the empty panes
Twittered - excited - full of zest.
The swallows always raised two broods
Of youngsters, three to six each time
In that open cup of mud and straw
Which drew them from a southern clime.
Swooped in and out to feed their young
Until autumn chill became the sign
To sit twittering excitedly
On the silenced telephone line
All restless, young and old alike
I guessed it would not be too long
Before one day they'd all be gone
The call of Africa too strong.

This year they'll find their home is gone,
Six houses built on the garage site.
I hope my swallows soon find a barn
In which to nest and rest at night.
Since thousands of miles each way to come
Must be nature's miracle of flight.

Joy Mullins

Looking Back 1920 - World War II

No radio to mar the peace,
Candles flickering in the breeze,
Iron gas lamps light the street,
Village bobby on his beat.

Rough chalk roads made of stones,
Smoke curling up from chimney cones,
Knee-length pants rubbing boys' legs,
Flat buttoned caps perched on their heads.

Shadowy figures could be seen
On the silent picture screen,
Red plush seats springing up at will -
Untuned pianos sounding loud and shrill.

Soon the war came - make do and mend,
Evacuees, food shortage, letters to send
To soldiers fighting far from home,
Helping them feel much less alone.

Bombs and blackout, coupons, queues,
Rationed clothes and utility shoes,
Furniture built from salvaged woods,
Cycle lights with thick black hoods.

Daring convoys bringing food,
Crossing seas in treacherous mood,
Dodging 'plane and submarine
Lurking in the depths unseen.

Is the world a better place
For greed and envy between each race?
Has the fighting been in vain
Or can man talk, and use his brain?

Kathleen C White

Gunslinger's Eyes

In my heart,
Lies the path of my calling,
Into darkness,
I carry the light,
Born to fate,
Ever rising and falling,
Ever watching,
Through gunslinger's eyes,

On my hip,
Is the badge of a legend,
Through the darkness,
I hold my head high,
All the years,
All the waiting has ended,
Finally looking,
Through gunslinger's eyes,

To my path,
I am true as the arrow,
From the darkness,
In triumph I ride,
But the light,
Has receded to shadow,
In the depths,
Of my gunslinger's eyes.

Mark Cobbold

Special Eyes

In your eyes I see your soul.
Which are you - cruel or kind?
As the past years take their toll,
Can you see or are you blind?

Aliens never have eyes
Because they don't have a soul.
Intellect personified,
A life-form without a goal.

In your eyes I see a tear,
Enough to break my hurt heart,
Slowly breaking chains of fear
As each steel link begins to part.

In your eyes I see my pain,
As reflections in a glass,
Hurting me to hurt you again
As these moments slowly pass.

Jesus must have eyes like yours,
He did not people repel.
He opened so many doors
For the people loved Him well.

For ev'ry tear shed for me,
For ev'ry prayer for me said,
God grant me His strength to be
Living and free and not dead.

Winifred Rickard

DIANA (QUEEN OF HEARTS)

Quietly, you came into our lives, with such a gentle touch.
How were we to know that you, would come to mean so much.
The light that shone when you were there, a glimmer in the dark.
Like a flame that lights a candle, you were the first bright spark.

Your beauty and your kindness, your thought and loving care.
Your love and your compassion, you gave that all might share.
No one was too lowly, as you visit every land.
The ill, the poor, the lonely, you gave a helping hand.

You had problems of your own, (another they'd destroy).
Ignoring them, you harder worked, giving hope and joy.
You trimmed your mind, refuelled your heart, and brightened up your smile.
Then shining like a brilliant star, you made our lives worthwhile.

All life's major burdens you carried like a cross.
Now that you're gone we've yet to know, the fullness of our loss.
Cut down in the prime of life, beside the River Seine.
The light is out, the dark returns, and only hurt remains.

Tony Fuller

WINTER

Sparkling gold penguin
Wobbling and flopping.
Purple glittering snowflakes landing.
White bear skipping.
Silver and gold holly dancing.
Joyful children playing.
Gold and silver robin flying.
Shiny rain dropping.
White whistling wind swaying.

Alysha Paton (9)

Sand

Are you strong?
- be strong, there's nothing wrong with the song,
it's just that not everyone's singing along!

It's no good frowning . . .
you'll end up drowning,
- sucked down in a current of fears!
You'll rise for a while . . .
in the cold viscous bile,
- but remember each river has weirs!

So fasten your armour . . .
and buckle your sword
- for the moment of truth is at hand!
For your dreams and your life . . .
and your laughter and strife
- are no more than a handful of sand.

Warren Tombs

On Choosing A Hat

It was a very serious business choosing a hat,
She didn't like this and she couldn't wear that.
Black wasn't right and neither was blue,
She tried on heaps of each different hue.
A white with a veil - a pink with a daisy,
Yellow with spots - she fair drove us crazy!
A lovely green felt, with a little brown feather,
We went on and on, it seemed to last forever.
Cream tulle with lace, mauve, purple and grey,
What bliss to have time to shop all day.
Look! This red one will do 'cos it matches my socks,
Haven't we had fun Gran - with your dressing-up box!

Yvonne Catling

CULTURE OF CONFORMITY

Constrained by a
Culture of
Conformity and
Cut off from
Changing civilisation,
Conservative
Complacency is
Concentrated at the
Church fête
Celebrations but
Concealed behind the
Coffee cups and
Crocheted cuddly toys on
Crimson and white
Checked-cloth table
Coverings, their
Conceited
Conversations
Consist of tales
Constructed
Concerning the
Culling of
Cubs. Where is the
Conscience in this
Culture of
Cruelty?

Sue Johnston

SIDMOUTH

Well here we are in Sidmouth,
Oh! What a lovely place.
There's such a feel of crinoline and
perhaps a touch of lace.
The houses are so dignified and
some have oval plaques,
Recalling previous owners and
interesting facts.
A walk along the promenade, a
saunter not a race
Till we come to where the cricket's
played at such a gentle pace.
The gardens decked in summer flowers
No penny-pinching here,
Or visitors on the pavements drinking
umpteen pints of beer.
Oh if only all our summer spots could
return to this idea.
No brash array of dazzling lights,
No noisy arcades here.
Just the simple act of visiting and
a relaxing tray of tea
As our eyes are drawn across the beach
and gently out to sea.

Richard Plumley

MALTA

Sun, kissed the island
To welcome its visitors to
Landscapes, coves, rocky inlets
And golden sands.
You discover houses that mellow honey
Coloured against the blue sky,
Magnificent churches whose windows
Shimmer in the day's sun
Cast mosaic patterns on stone floors.

Knights once roamed Malta's rich
Land where long-haired sheep and
Goats graze.
Brightly painted fishing boats
Float on water's edge
And
Fishermen unload their nets
At the quay side.

J M Stoles

THE MILLENNIUM

The year 2000 was a far off year
And yet it's here
And old one for me, but never for some
Brand new lives appear, they've just begun
'Emily' is born, perfect, complete
Innocent, adorable, tiny hands and tiny feet
Adored by her parents, grannies and aunts
Uncles and grandads, that's where it all starts
Love from above and love all around
When it's finished in this life,
In the next 'twill abound.

Margaretta Story

Le Landes

Wander like an albatross,
I wonder where else to roam,
Free as a cloud I hang-glide,
Over the rocks and shale,
I make the pleasant journey,
With breathless panting glee.

Step upon a sleeper built bridge,
Overlook the sponge marsh reeds,
And the landscape without trees,
At the top of the valley with the sea ahead,
Scattered ruins here and there,
Who could wish for less.

Drawn to mounds in rolling clumps,
Gorse creep upon the trodden path,
Which skirts the cliffs,
Leading your eye to sister islands,
Speckled on the distant horizon,
To tempt your reach afar.

A Lagadu

The Wedding

Long slim fingers,
A band of gold,
Oath taken to have and to hold.
A few tears, love in their hearts,
Joy and happiness, till death us do part.
Organ playing here comes the bride,
And now a husband by her side.
Love and devotion, who could ask for more,
With a life in front of them for evermore.

Glennis Stokes

Death Of A Piano

The sun and moon shine on its face exuding an ebony glow
It stands alone and someone says
'That piano's got to go'

The piano's got to go my friends, it has no place in here
Now we must kill the thing we hate
And no-one shed a tear

It's been too long in pride of place ignored, unplayed, you know
Despite its strength and our disgrace
That piano's got to go

For we all hate what we cannot do, we 'play' and people jeer
We will destroy this thing we hate
The price is not too dear

The murder goes ahead at pace with jemmy, sledge and bar
Then someone shouts with contorted face
'Stop! You've gone too far'

I'm committed now, how can I stop? I groan for I feel pain
I turn and stare, the crowd look on
Their faces show disdain

They show disdain to the one they love, who destroys the
thing they hate
They seek assurance from above
Fearful of their fate

The timbers split, display fresh wounds, the heart and soul appear
No touching light of a silver moon
Will grace the keyboards here

The splinters fly and ivory cracks with every hammer blow
A whisper trembles from the back
'That piano's got to go'

Grotesquely lies the shattered corpse, it did not want to go
We stand in silence and remorse
We loved that piano so

Ken Todd

LEAN ON ME

Sometimes the world can seem an unpleasant place,
sanity drifting without a trace.
Look through the fog of doubt and see,
I'm waiting there for you to lean on me.

With fear in heart or stifled pride,
facing the truth can be an awful ride.
From the darkness of despair you must look to see,
I'm waiting there for you to lean on me.

I will wait here forever for you to lift your head,
from the people who hate or the things you dread.
Just look through the tears of pain and see,
I'm desperate for you to lean on me.

I know when you're hurt, I feel your pain,
when outside it's sunny but in your heart is rain.
Don't think this is how it's meant to be,
I can make things better if you lean on me.

I am not here to criticise or to judge,
I would never laugh, wink or nudge.
I can make a lot of differences to your life you'll see,
but first you must trust to lean on me.

John Hewins

Rain And Shine

Why is it raining, always raining?
Why do the clouds shed tears?
Flooding the countryside around us
Causing so many fears?

Why is the sunshine always hiding?
Why won't it come out to stay?
There's one spot of rain on the windowpane,
How long will it stay that way?

We've had the rain,
We've seen the floods,
Maybe the sunshine will come to stay
But there's one spot of rain on the windowpane,
How long will it stay that way?

Dulcie George

Our Millennium

The new year has begun;
All the songs have been sung;
Parties and fireworks are but memories,
Now life has begun,
Promises have been given,
Whether spiritual or material,
As the spring bulbs appear
Our futures will become clear,
This is a time for great cheer -
The veil will become clear -
That we may see through -
With great joy and jubilance
The whole year through.

Norma Pusey

On The Day That We Left

On the day that we left an earthquake struck;
A crack of distance separated home.
My tears were bullets;
With a trigger shooting uncontrollable pain.
A flock of fawns trampling memories;
Bound together by the passing of time.

I am the empress of goodbye grief.
I am the messenger bringing back the past.

Trying to fathom the future, whilst combating insecurity.
My disappointment took a backward roll;
Twisting and turning like a tornado;
Following a pathway to destruction . . .

On the day that we left a chapter of a book closed;
Now covered in dust,
Lay Untouched-Innocent-Precious-Memories.

Helen Saunders

For Anne

For me there can be only one,
I've loved her from the start,
I hope that she loves me,
If not she'll break my heart,
I've known her for so many years,
Through lots of laughs and lots of tears,
I love her more than words can say,
I need her more and more each day,
My life I know would not mean much,
Without her tender loving touch,
With her I want to spend my life,
I'm glad that she is now my wife.

K J Wood

A War Child's Lament

Oh Papa, please tell me a story,
A tale of a land far away,
Where the fairies live down by the river,
And they play with the children all day.

Oh Papa, please tell me a story,
Let me hear your strong voice once again,
Tell of sunshine and lovely clear water,
Where there isn't any sorrow or pain.

Oh Mama, please sing me a lullaby,
Please sing me to sleep in your arms,
Let me savour the warmth of your bosom,
Mama, let me feel all of your charms.

Oh Mama, please tell me you love me,
Oh Mama, please dry all my tears,
Please tell me that life will get better,
Oh Mama, please douse all my fears.

Oh Mama and Papa, I'm frightened,
Tell me, why are you lying so still?
Tell me, why are your eyes never open?
Tell me, why are your bodies so chilled?

Oh Papa, I can't hear your stories,
All I hear are the bullets so loud,
Oh Mama, your smile has now faded,
I'm alone and so lost in the crowd.

Oh Papa, I pray it will finish,
Oh Mama, I pray when I die,
That we'll all be together in heaven,
In that beautiful place in the sky.

F W Cumbes

TAKE IT TO JESUS

(Mark II : 1-7)

If you read Mark II
There you will see -
Jesus had travelled
To Bethany
He sent two disciples
To a village nearby
To fetch a wild colt
For the Saviour to ride.

To Jesus they brought it
Untamed and wild
But one touch from the Master
'Twas submissive and mild -
We too need the Saviour
On life's restless wave
From tempest and torrent
Only - Jesus - can save.

Temptations are many
In this world of sin -
There's only one answer
'Tis Jesus - stay close to Him
His mercy is boundless
His riches unknown
He never will fail you -
Never leave you alone

What a friend.

Maizie E Davies

Tim

We've got a new baby come to stay
But where he has come from I cannot say,
I must not shout or make a noise,
But must play quietly with my toys.
Especially when he's fast asleep,
Because when he wakes he starts to weep.

Mum and Dad don't play with me
Like they used to after tea.
They have to spend their time with him,
They call him Timothy I call him Tim.

I suppose perhaps he is rather sweet,
With his tiny hands and tiny feet;
But how I wish that he would play.
Mummy said he will one day,
When he's grown as big as me,
Goodness knows when that will be.
Oh isn't everything a bother
When you've got a baby brother!

Phyllis Ing

The Gruesome Grebs

Of the gruesome grebs be wary
That lurk beneath your bed
They're small, yellow and scary
And waiting to be fed.

He lurks among your clothes and books
His teeth are sharp and blue.
He'll grab your foot when the owl hoots
And it will stick like glue.

He'll pull your hair and squeeze your hearts
He'll break your bones and back
He'll rip and tear you right apart
He'll stuff you in a sack.

Beware when you next go to bed
In your room grebs might be.
So remember what I just said
You wouldn't want to be a pea.

Samantha Whiting (11)

IMAGES OF ANGER

See pink

Build up a
Resentment
A scowl lays bare
The message sent.

See orange

Leads to great
Unrest
To fume at things
That you detest.

See red

Explode into a
Rage
Reach boiling
On the temper gauge.

See anger.

Karen Jones

Rainbows

Is loving me too dangerous?
Is it more than you can bear?
Were you hurt beyond redemption?
Do you think that you daren't care?
Though the scars are etched so deeply
You fear you'll never lose the pain
If you'd only let me love you
I could help you love again

Does it scare you to be normal,
To take it daily, step by step?
Build a love on trust and friendship
And laughter and respect?
We have these things already
So you see, we're halfway there
If you could only let yourself
You would see how much I care.

Will you always compare me to her?
Do you think I'll hurt you too?
Don't you know we could be happy?
I am nothing without you.
But until you take that first step
And learn to trust again
Where others can see rainbows
You will only see the rain.

Annie Zac

Calling Out To One Another

I know I've known you before in times gone
etched in centuries rather than days.
Long moments passed in terms of kings
stone formed by heat now coldered by rains
lasting briefly in extinctions and formations
of animals too beautiful to wait until we arrived again.
I see inside myself
moments you held me in times warmer than these
nights frozen held back by your arms
dates carved high on buildings
now raftered to skies and immortal wind
though memory eroded by rebirth and death.
I feel again over and over
those sunshined days of light and earth
when I was your dutiful son
strong protective father
your brother, lover,
sweet holding mother
and
finally betrayer.
You forgave me all of these
as I must forgive you too
though now I need end of intertwining paths
destinied remeetings
this everlasting foreknowledge
in place of choice.

Neil Benbow

HOLDING ON TOO TIGHT

There were times when I felt so lonely,
There were times when I felt so sad.
There were times you were my one and only,
There were times we shared . . .
How could they turn so bad?

Darling, I must go now,
Because love no longer stays.
I tried so hard to see your point of view,
But lost count of the days.
I loved to have you near me,
We're holding on too tight,
But now I know
I've got to let you go
Because sadness won the fight.
I guess I was right.

There were times when I felt like hating,
There were times when you were so cold.
There were times when you just kept me waiting,
There were times I cared.
How could this dream grow old?

Darling, I must go now,
Because love no longer stays.
I tried so hard to see your point of view,
But lost count of the days.
I loved to have you near me,
We're holding on too tight,
But now I know
I've got to let you go
Because sadness won the fight.
I guess I was right.

Peter Steele

A Misty Morn

As I climb to the highest point, I look down, far below.
The sun is shining brightly up here, creating an ethereal mist,
swirling gently, covering the valley, no wind to blow.
Under that soft white blanket, what is hiding there, what
pastures green.
As the temperature rises slowly, soon all will be seen.

'Tis only then I shall be able to see for miles and miles,
for the valley will be clear.
The mystery of the moor holds close its wiles,
as the sun casts huge shadows, making a strange atmosphere.
I feel quite alone as I stand high upon the Tor, tho' I know
that others must be here, my gaze intent as I eagerly
wait for more.

If I close my eyes I can almost feel I can touch the sky,
as the scene below begins to change, the mist rising
slowly, all becomes clear.
What beauty my eyes behold, as green fields with cattle
grazing unfolds.
A tiny church upon a distant hill, a hamlet tucked away.
The lives of another species, for them just another day.

I wonder, do they take for granted this glorious scene,
for I as a visitor, a different being live in a city,
cramped and with no style.
I shall feast my eyes upon the valleys and hills,
the wild ponies, the bird-song, to enjoy as I will.

I will return again to this wonderful place,
where there is no haste.
But for now I will stay and just ponder a while.

Helen Phillips

TIME THE DECEIVER

Be not deceived by that traitor called Time,
Though his bounty seems boundless, his patience sublime.
He pretends all our burdens he'll bear till the end:
A sweet tempered, amiable, flexible friend.

If you *beat* him or *mark* him you'll cause him no pain;
You can *spend* him or *waste* him - he'll never complain
You may seek to *kill* Time, you'll not end up in Hell;
You may even *do* time; time only will tell.

Some of his habits give rise to a rumour
That Time has a morbidly keen sense of humour;
For he dawdles when no one is having much fun,
But when good times appear, he breaks into a run.

So rely not on Time; of his friendship steer clear,
For he's cruel and relentless, a villain to fear.
He's always at mischief, he's never at rest,
And he's most to be feared when life seems at its best.

Though he fills empty heads and makes fools feel they're wise,
He will addle sound minds and he'll weaken keen eyes.
He will seize up strong joints till he slows down your pace
And he'll carve ugly lines in the skin on your face.

He will pluck out your hair, or make it turn grey,
For each gift that he offers, you finally pay.
He nurtures fair women, makes strong men out of boys;
Though he flatters us all . . . in the end, he destroys!

Norman Ford

Almighty Music

In snow-white robe, God the creator
Held meeting, important concert, name date.
Sternly 'We will have no fighting, arguments.
United we will show our continuing faith.'

'Host of Angels will sing' my blue heaven.
Deaf Cuffbert do your best, be in tune.
Few in crowd, whisper 'He will spoil choir.
When Christians celebrate 2000 years soon.'

Brass band led by demons, to blaze away
Welsh gathering pluck away on harps.
Archangel Gabriel will toot his horn
Trumpets loud notes shrill lemon sharp.

Winged animals fly to flight of bumblebee
Thunder and lightning polka, bellowed by Thor.
Tiny pretty angels, sugar plum fairy dance,
Chariots race to exciting 1812 Overture.

Devil struts 'Oh Baby light my fire.'
Amazing Grace. Smart, Scot bagpipe band
Irish Hum 'Danny Boy', try not to weep.
Bread of Heaven. Harmonize by football fans.

Lazer beams flash, swirl evening sky,
Seven sisters, Milky Way, twinkling display.
Moon resplendent wearing golden halo,
Heaven aglow will end our celebration day.

Phyllis Smith

Dawn Chorus

At dawn
the sun escapes
from the prison barriers
of the night
and stains the morning sky
with its blood red arrival
until at last
the power and force
of the flaming star
marks the beginning
of a brand new day.

At sunrise
all the feathered creatures
of the sky
join in the chorus of the dawn
when their song of praise
rises higher and higher
in the chill morning sky
thanking the solar star
for the heat and life
it bestows upon the Earth . . .

and then it rained . . .

Stephen Gyles

None To Impress

This time I believe I'll lose you for good,
Another day, a row, what happens now?
It's time to close this account I guess,
Affair turned out the only way it could.
And from it I will escape with a bow,
You are not the only one hurt I stress.

My part of this affair's not been explored,
Never thought love would end, don't want a row.
Looking back we didn't buy much, I digress,
Quickly you changed, I thought I was adored,
Now I've none to impress.

S Mullinger

Tropical Storm

Over the sea
The white spray came
Whipping inshore on the reef
Against the ebony background
Of sky and clouds
Lightning reached out
Joining sky and sea together
Turning clouds vivid reds and purples
Sand whipped by the wind from the beach
To cut the skin like small razor blades
Stinging eyes
Palm trees bending in the wind
Sending its fronds
Flying through the air like spears
Coconuts hitting the ground
Breaking into many pieces
Trees kissing the ground
Their twigs and branches cracking and breaking
As its roots pull out of the sodden ground
To hang like a muddy octopus
On the end of the trunk
Rays of sunshine breaking through clouds
As the storm abates
And a new day begins.

Patricia Parslow

Dawn - Awake

Hail new morn as sun begins to rise
I now rub the sleep from dreary eyes
Look! Don't just glance at the sky of light
You sun peep at me, new start of day, new life.

All the miles you've travelled
As I've slept after my close of day
All the things you have seen
Hundreds and thousands of miles away.

But now I'll watch you for a while
As a day will follow this dawn
No two days are alike
Some much fun, others full of scorn.

Just make the best of every day
They start off fresh and new
Thank our God for every one
That's been given to you.

So watch that dawn as it breaks once more
No matter what time of year
All should be cherished
They make life more sweet and dear.

Now they are part of life's free gifts
The ones that are most sincere
So take time to watch as dawn breaks
It's here, every day, of every year.

Joy Cook

OUR COUNTY OF DEVON

I dare say we all think
Our county's the best
But I feel in Devon
Living here we are blessed
Surrounded in some parts
By deep rolling seas
Have beaches and rocks
Drake's island is seen
From the Hoe here in Plymouth
A wonderful view
The bowling green, Drake played
As the Armada was due
A walk to the Barbican
Fishing boats wait
A plaque showing where
The Pilgrim Fathers had sailed
We have so much history
Parklands, estates
There are stannery towns
Ever peaceful and quaint
The moors going for miles
With breathtaking views
Rugged unspoilt
You can go where you choose
It has beauty and mystery
Rolled into one
This county of Devon
Has always been home

Jeanette Gaffney

THE BIBLE'S SWEETEST PROMISE

Under the wings of Jehovah
Our world will live in peace
Under the command of Jehovah
Wars and ruin will cease
Under the laws of Jehovah
Children will grow and thrive
Under the justice of Jehovah
No one will be despised
Under the might of Jehovah
Satan will be abyssed
Under the thumb of Jehovah
He will never be missed
Under the power of Jehovah
Jesus will reign as king
Under the wisdom of Jehovah
We'll all rise up and sing
Then
Under the love of Jehovah
Paradise will begin.

Julie Workman

FAIRIES

I was awoken in the night,
There I saw a wonderful sight,
Dancing in the light of the moon,
Six little fairies were singing a tune.

Come out, come out and play with us,
Come as you are, don't make a fuss,
We come each night to play with you,
With blonde-haired girls we know there's two.

Up and down the moon we slide,
Over the stars we jump with stride,
Little windows we peep and see,
Tired-eyed children sleep peacefully.

Dawn is breaking, it's time to fly,
Back to our crystals and beds to lie,
Get some rest for another day,
When we will come to take you to play.

L James

RHYTHMS TURNING

When the dove begins to call,
When the night begins to fall,
When the day begins to wane
And the night takes up the strain,
Peace is near and quietness too,
Allowing life to start anew.
For through the night and darkness' cloak,
Other worlds appear - evoke,
The wisdom, weaving, stirring, teaching,
Dreams that tell us what we are reaching.
Taking turns in life's full stream.
Threading, threading angel beams,
Through the tide of evolving space,
Connecting stars - appointing place.
Day and night the radiant sun,
Shines alike on all, and one.
Around the world, where life begins
To seek its life, let go its sins.
So let the rhythms' turning pace,
Bring us to a place of grace.

Jean Hatherley

CANCER

In my heart I feel a tear,
In my mind I shed a tear.
No one to tell what I'm going through,
The hurt, the pain, the worry too.
Cancer has taken the man I love,
He's out of pain in heaven above.
It's my turn now to fight the disease,
Disfigured from the surgery.
People say how well I look,
But they don't see when I am not so good.
I try to be brave and face what comes,
But cancer frightens everyone.
Each day is a bonus to be embraced,
Each flower so beautiful at break of day,
As the sun goes down and stars appear,
I thank God that I'm still here.

S Raven

THOUGHTS

Decision begins by letting go,
loneliness ends by saying hello.

Wisdom begins by being aware,
misery ends when we share.

Peace begins in the mind,
worry ends when left behind.

Hope begins with a dream,
failure ends when it is seen.

Love is the beginning and the end,
hate is alone, without a friend.

T N McCarroll

Darkness Passing

The sun shone
Then it went grey

The sun went out, it's black today
Then it went cold no bird did sing
till the sun was eclipsed except a golden ring

The light became bright there's beauty in sight
and birds did sing majestic in flight

Life is like this a miracle it's true
so hold up your head when you're feeling blue

When cold and dark and lonely you feel
When battered and worn on bent knees you kneel

Remember the eclipse the miracle you've seen
And look to the future not where you have been.

James Thornberry

Homeless Nation

Homeless nation, children dying,
Tears keep flowing, never drying.
Young and old, troubled dreams,
Sleep won't stop the haunting screams.
Grieving nation, so forlorn,
Their only sin was being born,
Homeland pillaged, forced to flee,
Seeking out impunity.
Scattered nation, must not perish,
Hope is all you have to cherish.
Hope for peace to end your plight,
Hope for freedom, that's your right!

Dave Sloan

When I Met You

(Dedicated to Kelly Day 'an inspiration')

I was once in search of love
For the inner peace, carried on the wings of a dove
Alone, wishing for what I so often read about
Dry within, the worst feelings of a drought
When one night, that was all it took to realise
Meeting you, I saw a reflection deep within your eyes
The love I'd so long been searching for
Started to grow within me more and more

I am no longer in search of love
Now, I am sending my own on the wings of a dove
I cannot remember the sense of being alone
I have been set free - able to walk and roam
I owe this to you - for you showed me the way
You may ask what you did - to that I can only say
Your love for me brought me off my perch
But it is my love for you that ended my search.

Carl Haggerty

Care

Please don't leave me in this place,
They don't even know my name,
They call me Mrs Stevens,
But my real name is Jane.

I didn't mean to wet your chair,
I'm sure it's not a crime,
I never put you in a home,
When you would not stop wetting mine.

I don't like their plastic food,
Their plastic grins and smiles,
I won't be a Mrs S,
Halfway down their files.

Don't leave me in this awful place,
Take me home to die,
I promise I'll go quietly,
You won't even have to cry.

Ralph Collier

A FRIEND

The old oak tree has a tale to tell
Of anger, sorrow and love.
Many's the time I have sat 'neath her boughs
And looked at the sky above.
The question will you marry me,
Was made such a long time ago.
Love blinded my eyes I was so much in love
If only I had said no.
Years after I sat 'neath the old oak tree
Feeling sure that my life I'd wasted.
My anger and sorrow, no love left in me
The bitterness of love I had tasted.
The old oak tree became a steadfast friend
To tell all my troubles to.
A promise of love not to give or to lend
Never knowing one day I'd meet you.
My old oak tree has a new tale to tell,
Of happiness, laughter and love.
Don't dwell on the past or of love gone before
Reach for the sky up above.

Sheila Trim

Bluebells

Velvet carpet, rippling, swaying;
 Royal blue and purple, laying
Like a violet coverlet
 Over morning hedgerows, wet
And sparkling, fragrant too;
 Matching skies of summer blue.

Vases overfilled with blueness;
 Spiky emerald leaves and newness.
Perfume of my childhood days,
 Filters through my memory's haze.
I wander through the bluebell beds:
 A thousand bobbing, nodding heads.

A blowing blueness comforts me,
 So many far ahead to see.
Careful though I am at treading,
 A trampled trail behind me spreading;
Behind me stirring, picking at, blueness.
 Ahead, much better, bluer newness.

Baskets laden and still more,
 Adorn and colour woodland's floor.
Walking mothers, children skipping;
 Talking children, mothers picking.
Endless carpet; on forever;
 Pity tiny bells should wither.

Dainty freshness, gone too soon.
 So long to wait until next June.

Shirley Arnold

OLD SAYINGS AND SUPERSTITIONS

If a black cat should cross your path
Then lucky you will be,
But walk beneath a ladder
And bad luck you will see.
If too many cooks can spoil the broth,
I wonder why it should be
That many hands will make light work,
It doesn't make sense to me.
Sad is the wooing that's too long adoing,
That is what they say,
But marry in haste, repent at leisure
For you will rue the day.
Three times a bridesmaid
But never a wife,
If you don't want trouble
Never stir with a knife.
A four leaf clover is lucky,
A white horse is lucky too,
But break a mirror and you will find
Seven years' bad luck face you.
Wash your face in May dew
And be beautiful all year.
Cure your ills by riding a donkey
Facing to the rear.
If you want to appease the devil,
Then you should say 'Touch wood.'
But does anyone really believe these things
Can bring luck bad or good?

Ivy Neville

In Memory Of Scamp

(Our best friend - 1987-2000)

You were our friend, we loved you so,
it broke our hearts, to let you go.

But we must think, of what is best,
we know that you deserved to rest.

So goodbye now our loyal friend,
who trusts in us right to the end.

We let you have your dignity,
your doggy spirit now runs free.

And in a place not far away,
where once again you run and play

I know that we will never part,
Your memory's kept within my heart.

Linda Palmer

Genesis

When summer's vibrant colour fades
And autumn paints more subtle shades -
Each season must its cycle run;
October's mist screen September's sun.

Migrating birds begin to gather,
Relay their leaving with anxious chatter.
Before the snow decides to fall -
And blow in drifts against the wall.

A hungry vixen sniffs the air,
To catch some creature, which unaware
Of being stalked while hunting too,
It's nature's style all winter through.

But winter cannot last forever,
Its grip will loosen, its ties will sever;
Soon southern winds bring softest rain -
It's time to welcome spring again.

Jean Stephens

THE GOLDEN YEARS

Freedom at last to come and go as we please
Retirement is here and it's like a soft breeze.
No clocks to watch or time sheets to fill
Sally, Rosie, you and me with time to kill
It may sound dull but there's so much to do.
Sally and Rosie need 'walkies' too
Life goes along and we have the time
To sit, relax and enjoy a lager and lime
I cook, sew, paint and make bread
And you are busy with wood in the shed.
We've found this bungalow, large, airy and bright
With everything level, three loos, it seems right
Nestling amidst thatch, cob and countryside
With church, post office, pub and ten miles
From the seaside.
We've settled in Devon, a dream come true
Our hopes and plans grew and grew
Living near the Blackdown hills
This is our home, with flowers on the
Window sills.

Ruth Bell

SEASONS

Eternal round - the seasons come and go.
They do not cease and none can stop their travel.
All year through the weather alters landscapes and our moods.

Bird-song heralds summer days, long and lazy in the shimmering heat.
Crops that benefit from longer hours of sunshine strong,
Grow tall to feed both man and beast.
Vibrant colours that adorn the hedgerow supply a feast for any eye
that cares to look.
The mellow sound of ball on willow bat joins with the song of
skylarks soaring far above,
And cloudless skies lift spirits high.

The lengthening days begin to close in and lush green leaves
start turning brown.
When autumn comes the migrants leave for sunnier climes -
Away from the damp, cold days that soon must follow,
Whilst mammals hurry to feed on what remains
And stock their larders to keep them fed through hard winter months.
Blackberries picked now keenly turned into jam and pies.
The October gales seem to blow away our much cherished summer tan.

The short, cold days of winter bleak cause most to hurry home to
roaring fires,
To sit and watch the colourful glow with curtains drawn.
While outside, birds hunt for seed put out by kindly folk,
And hedgehogs lie dormant under mounds of rotting leaves.
Frosts and snow change green to white,
And leafless trees stand out like skeletons on hillsides bare.

Daffodil and crocus bulbs beneath the earth await the changing
temperature,
And soon green shoots begin to show and test the air -
Before they bloom to welcome spring with colours fresh.
A new and active phase is taken up by all,
As birds begin to search for places for their nests
And animals look out for food and mate.

The trees return to green once more with buds unfolding one by one.
Flagging spirits now, with winter passed, rise up with hope
renewed for all to share.
The seasons' changes, often unobserved but oh, so vital -
To ensure the year long cycle of rebirth and life.

Stephanie Linney

CHALK DREAM

The sea and the beach
found me walking
somewhere between night
and full awakening.

Sand became cliff
high and menacing above
the narrow ledge
separating land from sea.

The shelf was smooth
white and slippery
from the spray of waves
whose tentacles snared my feet.

A being floated carefree towards me
arms outstretched, faceless
as a figure seen against the sun
and fearless of chalk and tide.

I moved gently towards it
to receive the message
merging with its embrace
at the start of another day.

David Firth

Hidden Beauty

Towards the moonlit glade, I silently stroll
hoping only to catch your midnight dance
sweeping aside leaf and fern, watching, waiting
will I ever witness such beauty again?

The shining radiance, of your slender forms
sensually moving to nature's rhythmic tattoo
an aura surrounding your very souls
enchanting beyond any man's dreams.

Sprite-like, in your elfin ways
hiding amongst nature's blanket
moonlight cascading upon your beauty,
enchanting me, holding me spellbound.

Where do you go, as daylight breaks?
Away from mortal man and all his sins
merging within Mother Nature's bosom
hiding from man's destructive presence.

As night falls, once more you return
yet, still your beauty eludes me
towards the moonlit glade, I silently stroll
hoping only to catch, your midnight dance.

David Strauss Steer

Creation

Midst the maelstroms of space and the parsecs of time,
The Almighty created equations sublime,
Gave the elements purpose, breathed life into matter,
Touched the stars into brilliance for Her fingers to scatter,
Moulded galaxies noble into vast array,
Scintillating in garlands like our Milky Way.

In the fullness of time She reviewed Her Creation,
Saw the beauties of Earth emerge from fulmination,
Seas pregnant with continents, vaulted heavens cloud-clad,
Appraising Her Work She rejoiced and was glad,
Yet from doubt and compassion a tear pearled in Her Eye,
As She fashioned mankind and then asked Herself, 'Why?'

Betty Gardner

The Monster

I bought a new cleaner the other day
Don't ask me why for I really can't say.
But the old one was getting past its best
So I thought it was time it had a rest.

The new one is perfect in itself
But as soon as I take it off the shelf,
The darn things shows me who is master
By tripping me up if I don't go faster,

It follows me round like a stupid dog,
Gets under my feet as I pull it along
By the great long hose like an elephant's trunk
It goes from side to side as if it was drunk.

When I tell the folks I am cleaning the place
They pull a very rude grimace.
'Visitors is it, coming to stay?
My word you'll need your skates on today.'

But I'll master the brute if it's the last thing I do,
Even if I live to be one hundred and two!
But truth to tell it cleans so well
I might get to like it, who can tell!

Muriel Johnson

The White Rose

She stands serenely at the bottom of the garden.
There amidst the blues and reds and yellows,
She stands like the purest fairy ever seen
And sends a scent of perfume billowing through
The garden. It's easy to spot her
Among the gladioli and peony and iris
Because she's like a landmark fair, blossoming
With all the beauty ripe of an English summer.
All the virginity in one so pure is displayed
In the floral show as the Vestal Virgin
Shows the maidens round about how to shine sublime
At the height of the summer season.
What a delightful show for any garden,
A decoration for Love's hair and a fitting tribute
For a Yorkshire emblem.

Thomas W Splitt

Acts I, II and III in Devonshire

Free-wheeling down the sunlit lanes
Of Devonshire's dream delights:
A schoolboy feels his pulses pound
With summer seasons' sights.

In calming forties, still the boy
A middle-aged man recalls -
Feeling once more that searing flame,
Those thrusting spurts of joy.

But - old men seldom feel that way:
Their night is far too near;
Stir winter's leaves with feeble feet,
And, silent, brood and stare.

Richard Flemington

The Sword

In our loft in the dark, away from daylight's eyes,
At rest in its scabbard it silently lies;
Its dull edge unhoned as never before
From its glory days when sharpened for war.

And did this relic from another age
Cut its mark on to history's page?
Or carried only for ceremonial show,
All polished and shining for military glow?

Crafted to kill and battles fight
And in the hand to balance right;
To thrust, to stab, to wound and maim,
Its strength and advantage the soldier's gain.

Was it a gleam of steel in the battle's roar?
Did it defend the guns of the Royal Artillery Corps?
On rampart or ridge of a Sebastapol hell
Amid cutlass and lance, grapeshot and shell.

Did it jab or cut, injure or hack?
Did it defend and repel any Russian attacks?
Was it ever stained with blood or dripping with gore
From engagements long past, in the Crimean war?

Oh! What stories this fine weapon might tell.
Was it brandished to fight with death screams and yells?
Its serrated edge able to rip
The guts of a man by twisting the grip
When face to face and blow to blow,
For England, against Queen Victoria's foes.

So sleep pointed blade, your very presence can tell
That whatever your actions, I'm sure you served well.
Be in peace in the darkness with your hardened steel cold.
Your life and your secrets to remain forever untold.

Eric Last

THEY

Who are *they,* the faceless ones
The people with a lot of power
They can cause such misery
As lesser folk they would devour

It's *they* say this and *they* say that
It must be right if *they* say so
No one really knows them
They keep their profiles low

They have a lot to answer for
In this world today
Life was much simpler in the past
Before *they* had their way

Try to rise above them
Don't let them take command
Ignore their chat and you will find
They can do no harm

It's all within the mind my friend
No one knows their names
Perhaps it's only make believe
Just a silly game

Don't give it another thought
Dismiss it from your mind
You'll do yourself a service
As well as true mankind.

Verity Denton

How Can I *Not* Love You?

How can I *not* love you?
Oh sweet one of mine
You say and do, the right things
At the right time.

You stick close to me
In times of unrest
And now in my life
You give to me the best.

How can I *not* forget,
Your patience, you show towards me
This is how you show
Your love towards me.

Happy young man
As I think of my girl
I love you so much
I think you can tell.

Thank you young lady, in loving me so
I need to be near you wherever you go
You're the one, I care for most
Because it's in your name I make my boast.

Oh, how can I *not* love you
Sweet one of mine?
My heart will love you
Till the end of time.

Perry K Leo

MY KITCHEN

There is furniture in my kitchen
Once belonged to someone else
A vase of flowers stands on the draining board
bright in the gloom.
The rayburn makes a dust which clings to
the picture rails,
The table is littered with dirty cups
The ashtray overflows.
The dog food sticks to the faded pink
carpet.
In the corner lies a pile of boots.
Boots for walking, boots for riding,
boots for work.
In the other corner stands a chair
with a pile of washing on it.
The cupboards are full of food and junk.
There are dogs under the table in the kitchen
But I wish I could stay in my kitchen
instead of going to work to pay for it
I like it in my kitchen.

Lin Fortune

MAY NOT A POET MAUNDER?

O lovely fruit, well past thine harvest now.
Was it some old bucolic man of soil
Or was it some sweet maiden, hot from toil
Who plucked thee in thy prime from off thy bough?

Perhaps thou heeded not that parturition;
I doubt thou felt much pain nor even fear -
Sensations that in mankind bring a tear,
Reminding us of death if not perdition.

Oh, didst thou feel the sun which made thee swell,
Those soft, sweet zephyrs, mercy's gentle rain
That fell from heav'n above to parched terrain?
I hope thou didst but thou wilt never tell.

O lovely fruit, O most delicious boon
(To poets who shout, 'To Bathos he'll descend!'
I answer 'Pish' and also 'God forfend.')
I love thee, wrinkled, meek, prosaic prune.

Frank Sutton

GERBERA

(For a friend)

The last tears of dew
drawn off green leaves dappled shaded,
encroach dry thirsty earth with a ping
and disappear in a million particles.
The sun rids innuendoes of summer
on a warm sultry breeze
as it flickers dancing flames
of orange singed petals.
Sparks ignite passion,
a burning cascade of colour
attracts naked woman out into the garden.
Bodies soak sun with a glistening glow,
amid the tall stems of gerberas
that skirt cobbled walkways and gravel paths,
singing sweet ballads as they sway to and fro.
Till the warmth of bouquets encircle your breasts
like a life-long lovers' passionate breath.

A Cartlidge

IT'S A FUNNY OLD LIFE

Life is like an escalator, it has its ups and downs,
We often feel unhappy when we've no one around.
When friends no longer keep in touch
And loved ones rarely stay,
When family quarrels become too much
And relatives move away.

We sit all lonely, sometimes sad,
Reflecting on good times we had.
As teardrops glisten on our cheeks
We ponder what to do.
Just this once, a spark of hope
Of meeting someone new.

But life is also like the sun,
It's bright and warm with endless fun.

The treasured memories of the past,
The nights we drank and danced and laughed.

The times we giggled with our friends,
The nights we wished would never end,
That morning after that's always the same
With those immortal lines 'Never again!'

So we really should be feeling glad,
That life's been good and not that bad.
For in this world many people suffer
With countries at war destroying each other.
Innocent children left on their own,
Their families left dying, no food and no home.

So the next time we moan and make a fuss,
There's people out there far worse off than us.
So let's try to forget our trouble and strife
Smile and be happy, it's a funny old life.

Michael Page

ROADY DRIFTER

The road runs ever on, ever on,
Mingled shades of green in a still quiet aloneness,
Times of crowded rooms and roads,
But my ears do not hear, my eyes do not see,
Silence surrounds me.

Tapestry carpets of woven leaves,
Golden meadows, silver trees,
Tunnels of trees and leaf-framed images
Meadow cows graze to the song of the birds.

Cross-legged dirty feet amongst dewy-grassed clover,
Eternal time turns over,
Beautiful peace, elusive serenity.
Oneness with all, for all eternity.

But then I'm stood by a roadside, hair in my eyes,
Bad stares because they are not I.
Weary worn limbs, tired torn clothes,
The sun in my face, the sun in my soul.

The jukebox cafes, music beats out at me,
Goes through me, is part of me,
Tea-ringed tables, one cup lasts an hour
Sun through the windscreen, hot on my face,
Parting tears forgotten will leave no trace.

I see the steeples, they have no meaning,
People imprisoned within themselves.
A radio drums to the sound of the road,
Thought moves on to become a memory.

Who to meet next, a devil, a demon, a prince or a poet,
Where to go, who to see, what to do, who to be,
So many people waiting to be known, so much love to be shown,
Cars pass me by and by, some stop and ask of me the reason why?

Pamela Hayhurst

A Place Of Quiet Reflection

Obscured by mist yet highlighted by sun,
The abbey stands in ghostly shape and form;
Fine windows now exposed to air
No longer echo chanting prayer
Or harmony of minds in unison
In praise of God, to whom those souls were drawn.
Whilst elements predate these structured bones,
The prayer still lingers deep within the stones.

Exchanging notes, our sense of awe expands
Revealing life contrived to be austere,
Where harsh regime within, confined,
Plays havoc with the modern mind.
Such selflessness is hard to understand
Since we no longer bow to threat or fear;
Yet whilst we dwell upon those distant days
A silent presence filters through the haze.

The aura captivates our consciousness
Inviting us to seek these consecrated sites;
These archetypes of Heaven's Gate
With ambience to meditate.
This open-plan now filled with emptiness;
This place of quiet reflection bathed in light
Perpetuating faith on firm foundations,
Uniting souls through countless generations.

J M Redfern-Hayes

Happy New Year

How long is it since he was born
Two thousand years, well more or less
The calendar has been altered
Never mind we will have to guess

He told us to expect the worst
War and pestilence and so on
We preferred the cheerful story
See you all next year in Zion

Genetic food for the starving
Give BSE to healthy cow
Give AIDS not aid to Africa
Don't worry about pollution now

The Dome is built on poisoned ground
The treatment should make it alright
If it glows in the dark, who cares
Now it's paid for the outlook's bright

There's not much in it about him
Cause nobody wanted to pay
For anything you cannot sell
It is out of place on the day

We will have a long holiday
Or little work with lots of pay
Do it the New Century Way
Or will four horseman spoil the day?

John M Spiers

VILLANELLE

My garden had a secret to disclose.
When summer came and all the world was green
Two lilies bloomed, the yellow and the rose.

In dreary winter how could I suppose
When pond lay dark, abandoned and unclean,
My garden had a secret to disclose?

Surely no plant survived the rake and hose,
But leaves float up and suddenly between
Two lilies bloomed, the yellow and the rose.

Under blue skies the willow leaned, to enclose
The dappled pond, as if it had foreseen
My garden had a secret to disclose.

Dragonflies, drawn to the water, chose
To flash and hover, while like king and queen
Two lilies bloomed, the yellow and the rose.

Much brighter flowers would soon their charms impose,
But I recall when, fresh upon the scene,
My garden had a secret to disclose:
Two lilies bloomed, the yellow and the rose.

Beryl Jenkyn

MUM AND DAD

You made me the person I am.
You taught me the meaning of life,
And whenever I felt afraid and alone,
You helped me through the strife.

You helped me through my good times,
And even through your bad.
That is why I love you both so much,
My life, my mum and dad.

Michelle Thorpe

Magic

There is a place not far from here
Magic beyond belief
Although it's only woods and fields
It brings me much relief

When I'm unhappy, stressed or sad
I go there right away
And everything which seemed so bad
Is righted while I stay.

O come with me and you will see
Exactly what I mean
Doubts and worries disappear
As if they'd never been.

This lovely meadow with its flowers
The woods where sweet birds sing
The hazel which became my bower,
The views and everything.

For me it's real enchantment here
No witch or magic brew,
But sounds of bird-song, peace and quiet
Tranquillity, rare and true.

Diana Price

City Nightmare

Screaming sirens, traffic fumes,
loud music blaring in the rooms,
rubbish littered street and park,
menace looming after dark.
Neon signs that dazzle eyes,
high-rise flats which hide the skies;
tawdry posters, sprayed graffiti
masking walls - 'tho not completely.
Grimy buildings, once so splendid -
whom, or what, have they offended
now to fall to disrepair,
rotting crumbling, dying there.
Is this squalor really rife
or just a part of city life?
Oh just let me hear once more
rollers breaking on the shore,
smell the sweetness of the hay
on the hills above the bay.
Never more I'll wish to roam,
cities? *No* - please take me home.

Brenda Heath

Pond Life

A blue dragonfly hovers over the weed,
The tadpoles wriggle like broken bead,
A sparrow splashes with obvious glee,
Then shakes to dry in the willow tree.

Pond skaters speed over the skin,
Making unseen tracks as they glide and skim,
Yellow king cups nod their heads,
As shubunkins swim near the water's edge.

A scruffy boot that's seen better days,
Laces undone, tongue awry,
Sits in the shallows, a sorry shipwreck,
Now is the home to a newt from the beck.

Shadows are lengthening, sun falls from the sky,
Now there's no sign of the blue dragonfly,
Then in the moonlight, a vixen and cub,
Drink the clear water, then forage for grubs.

Lynda Burton

THE JOURNEY

To walk a path without compassion,
Just a futile attempt
To extend an allotted space.

Like the arrest of a howling gale,
Like a flooded ocean.

The breath of life,
Simply fleeting moments,
In a race against time.

Like a migrant bird,
Like waves crashing on a shingle shore.

With grains of dust,
Thrown into a shelter of comfort,
Where life has turned a corner,
I saw a rosebud opening,
I heard a warbler singing, an orchestra playing,
Yes, how I loved the song!

Jane Rennie

PAINTED REALITY

Society corrupts the mind
And shapes my very soul,
So every day to keep at bay
I bear a shield of gold.

The real me is kept locked in chains,
Away from such a place,
Within this shell: a living hell
I wear a painted face.

It keeps away the bitter truth
Yet also keeps me down,
The light of day just fades away
Into a distant frown.

The deepest hope to me seems dead
And all the joy it gave.
Now every day I kneel to pray
Upon a baron grave

Rather than just tell a lie
My life became one too
But as a cost, my soul was lost
And all I have is you.

Nick Sawers (16)

THE DANCING

Come in your veiled beauty
And lead me to it.
Lift once more
The cloak of doubt from my shoulders
And I will fly with you to new pastures
And stay with you during the snowfall.

Hold my hand and we will tread footsteps
On the green blanket
Where the blades are blunt
And find a space between the stars
From where we'll look upon the world with eyes that see
And hearts that beat in rhythm to the dancing.

Rachel Packer

A Cheery Greeting

The dreariness of a wet December morn
Lifts suddenly with a flash of brilliant red.
Beady eyes fixed on kitchen window,
A crimson-breasted visitor sits on garden shed.

Such disdain shown at empty bird table
Washed bare by heavy overnight rain.
He flies down to inspect state of larder
Then retreats, hungry, to roof again.

The plight of this wee creature moves me,
His visit brings so much warmth and joy,
I desert the washing-up and tiptoe out,
Scattering titbits I hope he will enjoy.

As closure of kitchen door ensures his safety
He flies down, perching with glee
In midst of this enormous food mountain.
Such untold pleasure cock-robin gives to me.

The cheering effect of this crimson plumage
Warms me more than any winter heating
And through the grey dismal wintry days
I wait with anticipation for his greeting.

Pat Heppel

THE CLIPPERS' RETURN

It's ten long months since last we saw these yachts
in Plymouth Sound.
Since then the seven clipper yachts have sailed
the world around.
They've braved the mighty oceans in sun and wind and rain
Now crews and all their skippers are safely home again.
They'll soon forget the bad times and remember just the fun,
What memories they'll cherish of a task that is well done.
No matter who the winner is - or last to cross the line
They'll know that relatives and friends will think
they all are fine.
So raise your glasses for a toast to the skippers and the crews
Of the seven clipper venture yachts who gave us so much news.
Of life afloat and then ashore, as round the world they sailed.
Each one of them a winner not one of them has failed.

Gwyneth Futer

THE BOY IN MY CLASS

He sits in the corner, what he thinks nobody will ever know,
But we know his mum died long, long ago!
His round little face is very weak,
People shout, 'You scary freak!'
But I feel sorry for him when he moans,
No proper clothes, just skin and bones!

'You smell!' shouts a boy from the other end,
'I'll beat you up on the weekend!'
I mention no names but only 'boy',
The other boys play with him like a toy!
With only his dad and three other brothers,
No love in his life, not even any mothers!

But one day a new boy came to school,
To the sad boy he was not cruel,
Over he went and he made a friend,
They started talking and that was *the end!*

Samantha Sullivan (10)

To Sheena

If I were the wind that blew on Sheena's wings
I'd lift her up and help her soar away
We'd travel like a stone flung from a sling,
And circumnavigate the world in but a day.

I'd swirl and gambol round her feathered limbs,
Embracing all of her as I passed by.
She'd breast the storms and gales of many lands.
I'd help her tour the heavenly azure sky.

With Sheena I'd survey the continents below,
Investigating all the scenes that scurried by,
The deserts, mountains, seas and Arctic snow
And all the beauteous scenes that we could spy.

We'd travel on a moonbeam in the night,
And slip along the sunbeams in the day,
We'd revel in the everlasting flight
That lovers seek in their unending play.

I was that wind that blew on Sheena's wings
And pressed her gently to that world above
Together we experienced many lovely things
And brought them back, the spirits of our love.

Dymoke Jowitt

BREAKING FREE

I've done it at last, realised who I am.
Why I'm here, who I love, where I belong.
I've torn away from you - my terrifying past
That haunted me when I closed my eyes
No more guilt, no fear
All gone along with the 'friendship'
Hate lingers in my thoughts
It colours you black
Red is what you are - danger.
I thought I was in the wrong
At first, yes
You took my place, threatened me
Scared I went along
Guilt made me numb
Hate flooded my life, hate for me - and you
Physically you bruised me
Mentally you wrecked me
Now I'm free - why?
You pushed it too far, misunderstood me
You have nothing other than anger
I have freedom, my mind and thoughts are mine
No longer filled with hate for you
I survived - just
No one will ever scare me, not into 'love'
For I have peace, deep inside
Relief that you've gone
You'll never hurt me again
Nor haunt me
You are my past
I am my future.

L J Futcher

ECLIPSE - ACROSS THE YEARS

The most wonderful sight she'd ever seen
Took place on a field of Lancashire green.
The scientists came from farthest shore
And set up their tripods at her door.
The sky went purple with stars about
The day the sun was blotted out.
Shadows, colours swirled around,
She looked astonished at the ground.
She never stopped talking about the sight
When her day was turned to night.

My family gathered on Devon's green
But not a scientist to be seen!
And now it is my time to see,
My time to gaze on this majesty.
Light clouds were floating with patches of blue,
But those clouds closed up to obscure our view.
I stood deflated, I shook, I began to cry,
I would not see her purple sky.

And then, by magic, a gap in that sky
And the sun burst through with a patch on its eye.
Agog we gazed, the light going bleak,
And soon a mere scratch down the side of its cheek.
Then the stillness and the shadows came
And a pea green haze fell over our lane.
I sank in the darkness, the silence, the cold,
A curtain dropped on a cloth of gold.
And I heard Mother's voice inside my head,
Across the years though long time dead.

D M Cudmore

If I Had Three Wishes

If I had three wishes, whatever would they be?
Lots of fame and fortune, a life of gaiety,
Or to have such beauty, all heads would turn to me?
Or should I love forever, but where would my friends be?
These are three fine wishes, but are they really me?
No, I must start again to think my wishes three.

Man's needs are really simple, if only he could see,
Not to be so selfish, or live so ruthlessly.
Instead, let all the races live in peace and harmony.

If I had three wishes, I must not waste a one,
Just think so carefully, what really would be fun.
First, I'd like my sight returned, the world about to see,
Next to be with loved ones, such happiness and glee.
Then I must ask God's blessing, my life to carry on.

If I had three wishes, that is what they would be,
Man cannot buy the happy things,
They are God-given to thee.

Lillian Baxter

Pain

There are times when
No words
No science
Nor gentle caress
Can heal that special wound.

A wound that shows
No blood
No gore
Nor even scars
But one that feels most pain.

Pain that comes from in
The mind
The heart
Or whole body
That only time can cure.

Time matched with oneself
In thought
In action
In whole being
Will pull you into light.

Nicola Westell

Candlelight In A Sitting Room On A Stormy Night

Outside the storm does furiously blow,
But in the evening fireglow,
Soft romantic candlelight,
Flickering yellow light,
Burning bright,
On a stormy night,
Candle flame burning low,
Sending out a rosy glow,
Filling the warm and cosy sitting room,
From a vase of chrysanthemums in bloom,
Where they are pleasantly placed,
On the black marble fireplace,
With shadowy pictures of their flowers,
In the candleglow hours,
Candlelight burning tall,
By the side of the firelit wall.

M J Harris

A Journey

We travel on this planet
As it moves us round and round
An ever moving circle
With our feet on solid ground.
Our lives continue daily
With its pleasures and its pains
Each an individual
But facing the same strains.
For some the constant motion
Is a simple, easy ride
While others lose their bearings
And have to seek a guide.
To navigate the safest route
Where happiness reigns high
Some stand by their morals
While others cheat and lie.
But the circle keeps on spinning
No matter what we do,
And as we all grow older
We grow more wiser too.
The knowledge that we gain
As our ride through life moves on
Can only serve to better
Those who do us wrong.

Sue Yorke

OPPOSITES

The sea, the sea, the cruel, cruel sea,
so wild and unforgiving.
The sea, the sea, the cold, dark sea,
reflecting man's misgivings.
It's not the place for the faint of heart
and you pray to 'God' at the journey's start.

The sea, the sea, so dark and grey,
causing great foreboding.
The sea, the sea, with its ferocious way,
to all on it distraughting.
The fishermen harvest midst fear and dread,
too many to remember, too many dead.

The sea, the sea, the benign blue sea,
so soft and all-embracing.
The sea, the sea, the calm warm sea,
for frolicking and rejoicing.
It's just the place for fun and games,
and for all the fame of those well-known names.

The sea, the sea, a translucent green,
exciting and uplifting.
The sea, the sea, a beauteous scene,
its waves forever shifting.
It gives us life, an expanse to play,
to remember the sand and a summer's day.

Martin V Ullathorne

ETERNITY

So brief in passing,
how quickly shadows fall, building up years
of beautiful memories,
of passionate rage,
of silent suffering;
all for the desolate tomb.
How desperately we cling to life,
mesmerised by immortal smiles;
surely this can't be the end?
That unknown void to eternity leaves you doubtful, insecure.
Free your mind to belief and destroy the torment in your soul.

Our eyes turn to the standing stones
that mock us in our carefree hearts;
The lilies indifferent to their keepers,
the grass, with no respect, grows on.

Johanna Williamson

FRUITION OF A DREAM

I've wished for a dream that I longed to come true,
that day came when I met and got to know you.

From the moment I saw you I longed to be part of your life,
come happiness, sorrow, or periods of strife.

Life can hold so much by its very nature,
love and contentment being part of the adventure.

This journey we could make would hold no fears,
as the days turn into months and the months into years.

Won't you take a chance on this honest humble man,
who loves and cares like no other can.

Paul Davies

The House Has Fallen Down

This was a tale
Told from the length
Of a long table
And everyone's faces
Froze into icy stares,
Voices rose and fell
And echoed across the well
Where the water bubbled
Freely, as the sky could tell
Only the knell
Of the day's end,
When they all fled
From the lightest
Notes of the sound
Of the singing bird.

A lazy quiet whisper of sound
Rose against activity
Showing a distance
In revelation.
Uncanny leaves rolled
Together on swaggering
Branches, beloved curves,
Rocks and rich trunks
Coloured brown sweated,
None was described or painted
As words flowed into the
Passage of the stream
Like the song of the stars
Joining, quaking
And only sky words
Reigned centrally.

Juliet Fowler

The Gift

Sweet velvet face of a pansy
Myriad shades of a rose
Trees in their new spring green mantles
Icicles shine as they froze

Buds greet the world with the sunlight
Fields full of waving gold corn
Soft nose of sweet gentle Dobbin
Tiny lambs just newly born

Smooth sea reflecting the moonlight
Huge angry waves pound the shore
Ships sailing slowly to harbour
Families wait on the shore

Small children's bright happy faces
Kind well-loved eyes of a friend
River in spate or contented
Flows to the sea at its end

Thunder clouds menacing, angry
Lightning's flash lights up the sky
Peacock unfolding his glory
Birds teach their babies to fly

Beauty and grandeur and wonder
Things that bring fear or delight
Without it, all these would be missing -
Sweet blessed gift of my sight.

Enid Gill

Specific Ocean

'Hello, sea' I said,
Taking it by surprise,
As it tried in vain to avert its eyes,
'I'm busy washing away sand pies,'
Was the rather rude reply.

'Busy!' I said,
'Well that's a lie,
You'll ebb for an hour before you go,
And there is so much I want to know,
But your depths are far too low,'
And I turned and waved goodbye.

'Oh look!' said the sea,
'Where did you get the notion,
That I'm a sea and not an ocean,
Be like me and be specific,'
It was said with some emotion.

'What makes your mood so offhand,
You sound a little sick on land,
It's all that cream and contraband,
Or is that too simple for you to understand,'
I said, from the safety of the sand.

'Listen' said the sea with a sigh,
'Are you wearing those shorts for a bet?
And if you're afraid of the water,
May I recommend surfing the net,'
And *wet me without warning*.com/goodbye.

Malcolm Watson

ROMANCE

Is it true
What he just said
That love has gone
And romance dead.

That hearts and flowers
Don't mean a thing
No sounds of joy
With the birds of spring.

Say he lied
It's just a joke
A few choice words
Meant to provoke.

For what a life
Without romance
No moonlit walks
Or close up dance.

And without love
It must be said
That life has ceased
And we're all dead.

James L Wood

Land Of Delights

I live in God's own personal land,
A county endowed with sun, sea and sand,
Where the grass is green and the sky is blue,
The sun is warm and the people are too.
Visitors descend on us in their droves
And promptly purloin our loveliest coves.
When they depart and peace is regained
The relief we all feel is certainly not feigned.
I like to show off our scenery so rare
Also our flora and fauna for which we care.
In legends and folklore we're rich beyond belief
From sightings of the Beast of Bodmin we get no relief.
I believe it's there, as do many others too,
To get a decent photo of it would be quite a coup.
One important item all visitors have to try
Is the famous 'pasty', for which exiles heave a sigh.
Clotted cream is so tasty but, an enemy to the hips,
Try our wine - a finer nectar will never pass your lips.
Cornwall has so much to offer, if you care to look,
Not all our attractions can be found in the book.
I love my home and my good life in this county
And I love the land with all its bounty.
If you should visit our Duchy please treat us right
And help to keep this region always clean and bright.

Margaret Phillips

The Lonely Cow

I sit lazily in the field.
The world going by,
like every other day.
I can see ants crawling
between each blade of succulent grass.

They work together.
There is no boss and
no slaves, just workers.
They go about their business
building their homes.

I have no purpose to life
other than to provide milk.
Every one of them is needed.
They all belong to a chain,
but I am just a link that

can survive alone.
I sit in the field.
All alone
in a crowded field,
wanting to be part of the chain,

working with a team.
Rather than
sitting lazily in the field, all alone.

Jenny Masters (16)

The Adit

He went into the adit,
Crawling low along the old mine,
Deep into the old men's workings
And found -
The indented marks of the soles
Of hobnail boots in the rab cleave,
The curved horseshoe of the iron heel
Of the last miner to leave.

A narrow wooden wheelbarrow,
Encrusted with blue deposit
Of copper minerals from the drip, drip, drip,
From the seam above,
All preserved in the warm air -
A candle stuck with its own wax on a ledge,
An old square nail, an iron hammerhead,
An ochrous flaking wedge.

Wooden launders on the ground
Still flowing with running water,
Carrying it away to an open shaft,
Stalagmites and stalactites
Of blue copper and red iron residue,
Growing in the silent stream
Of never-ending drip, drip, drip,
Of seeping water from the seam.

Esme Francis

Cornwall

A land at the mercy of nature's whims -
Benign and serene if she feels forgiving
Though should she feel tempestuous then beware -
Seek shelter all things living.
For nature in her wrath can be awesome indeed,
Bringing frightening ferocious wind
Which boils the sea and batters the land
Building mountainous clouds so all beauty is dimmed.
But in a short space of time nature smiles once more
And golden fingers guild golden shores.
Spreading wide they encompass the hills and valleys
Pausing to softly stroke the wild untamed moors.
Then when the purple evening shadows start to meet
Sweeping away the tranquil hours
You will feel the ghosts of Cornwall's past pulse and beat
With their strange and mystic powers.
Yet when you wake tomorrow morning and gaze upon the sea
As the sun breasts the horizon's rim
All is different again, for no two days are the same
In this land at the mercy of nature's whims.

Paddy Jupp

Damnation

If we live
A meagre existence
Death is not painful
But for those
Whose life is righteous
Death is diabolical

Warren Brown

The Reluctant PCC

'We'll have a harvest supper,' the Vicar gaily said.
'Now, who's going to do it? Who will make the bread?
Who will buy the lettuce and who will buy the ham?
Who will buy the cheese and a big tin of spam?
Put your hand in the air and let me hear an aye.
Come on everybody, who will have a try?'
But they all just sat there and never said a word.
They all just sat there, as if they hadn't heard.

The Vicar tried again,.'Now who will make this spread?
We must have a leader, and be well and ably led.
Who will make an apple or a fine banofee pie?
Come on now, one of you, please have a try.
But they all just sat there and never said a word.
They all just sat there as if they hadn't heard.

'We'll need an entertainment for after they've been fed.
If you know a funny monologue, that could be read.
How about a song, or a conjuring trick or two?
The organist could tell some jokes, as long as they're not blue.'
But they all just sat there and never said a word.
They all just sat there as if they hadn't heard.

'Well,' said the Vicar, 'I'm all for diversity,
Instead of Harvest Supper, suppose we made it Tea,
And supposing that we said that all of it was free?'
'I'd come to that,' said the Vicar's Warden, Lee,
'And I would come as well,' said his wife, 'as long as it was free.'
The Vicar looked enquiringly, 'Who else would come?' said he.
'Oh me, and me, and me, and me.'
'Now,' said the Vicar, 'who will organise this tea?'

And they all just sat there and never said a word.
They all just sat there, as if they hadn't heard!

Catherine Hartland

In Time

Let me leave this life while I still
can walk the wharf on a winter's night,
and see reflected lights of houses, boats
        and harbour walls.
While I still can stroll the quiet streets
and say 'Goodnight' and take the hill
        toward my home -
yet turn and look and look and look again
and know with rising joy the town is mine.
How could I bear to merely sit or lie
and be unable to walk my space?
I know that mind and memory would serve me
        true and fine -
would take me down the hill and through
the streets toward my lighted place -
but not enough - no, never enough.
So let me leave before that time.

Mary Carver

Lovers' Dream

To rollerblade on moonbeams
Freefall on a summer breeze.
To land in a field of apple blossom
And dance to meet the dawn.

To stand naked on a river bank,
See the first streaks of sunlight
Light up your auburn hair,
As hand in hand we laugh, plunge in
To kiss, touch, display, just like the otters
As in their pool we play.

On cold winter nights
Sit before a blazing fire,
Sip a pleasing wine.
Then let soft lips search out,
And taste the fruits of love.

This the foreplay dreams of lovers
As two bodies merge, entwine,
Two hearts, two minds, as one.
Eternally.

A R Lewis

Eighty-Plus Miles 'Service'

I had a message from Martin,
Please bring some of your nonsense to read,
But my mind is beginning to wander
And become very empty indeed
I try to remember what I've written before
But my mind becomes very blank.
I've written and read what comes in my head
But now it's an empty old tank.
I've written of this and I've written of that
And bored you with ever so much.
You'll be glad to know that I'm beginning to slow,
And am really losing my touch.
Things will wear out I know you'll agree,
And my brain has never been 'serviced'
It's just had a rest from time to time,
After all I am nigh eighty-three.
So if I repeat anything I've written before
I know you'll be patient with me,
And think to yourselves that time hurries on
From this nonsense you soon will be free.

M Wevill

A Silver Dream And New Reality

Did you ever have a silver dream
Of an unexpected change in living,
Which the near future may bring,
With many celebrations in store,
Everlasting magic is included,
A splendour of contentment resulting.

This fantasy is exquisite,
Something very breathtaking,
A stunning effect of a wonderful feeling,
Which brightens a dull, daily existence.

But pure love is a unique human event
And has been noted from the beginning of time.
The heart's beat symbolises
An eternal affection and passion
Which is inspired by the true spirit of romance.

It is never too late to enjoy this experience,
Two people in love, in this, age is no limit.
A new feeling of tenderness,
With understanding and giving,
Company and unity in sharing,
Is always part of an infinite love,
A very desired outcome
And the result of a happy marriage.

Milly Saunders

The Field

As I enter the field the calm engulfs me.
Haven! This church of mine.
No stained glass windows encased by mortar
Lo! The river that winds and the bridge extends.
The island, the grass, the trees.
These colours cannot be matched by the artist's hand.

The aisle? The sweet carpet of grass that leads me on.
And the choir?
No human voice echoes aloft,
But the heavenly chorus of birdsong.
The altar? The vista that enlightens my soul.

I need no crucifix to remind me of my God here,
Only the trees,
As they gently wave their arms in the breeze.
The calm. The peace,
That one feels as one enters a place of worship
Lies here. It falls with the sun rays.

And I leave here with an inner peace.
All stress and worries gone.
I can leave this place untouched
Save for the breath of God.
Ready for the next worshipper.

I depart from my sanctuary, my church.
The field.

E Sanderson

A Moorland Spring

White clouds float lazily across an azure sky;
Buzzards mew plaintively above a nearby tor.
Small lambs run bleating to their mother's sides
And long-legged foals, ears pricked, gaze at the passers by.

The river Dart flows onwards to the sea;
Splashing o'er rocks that strew the river bed
And sunlight dances on the water cool
Making a myriad diamonds in the air.

Amidst the fragrant golden gorse,
New fronds of bracken push through peaty soil
And buttercups, bluebells and yellow tormentil
Bedeck the moorland's ancient floor.

A skylark soars into the air
And sings his precious song for all to hear;
And forked-tailed swallows swoop and dart
Catching small insects on the wing.

This glorious moor is once again awake.
Winter is gone and spring has come again,
Bringing new life and hope to all that dwell
In this a very special place on earth.

Ann Linney

The Call Of The Sea

The wild wild beauty of the sea
Pervades my soul where'er I roam,
I long to see the azure sweep
Of crystal glints, I must go home

To see the tumbling breakers foam
And waves come creaming o'er the sand,
And rock pools filling with the tide,
And smell the sea of my homeland.

The sweet sweet music of the sea
Calls out to me where'er I roam,
I long to hear the sound of waves,
Their endless beat, I must go home

To hear the sea in all its moods,
The soft sea sounds, or raging waves
With breakers crashing on the shore,
And thund'rous roaring in the caves.

My Island home, I must go back,
The blazing sun, the blue blue sea,
The sparkling air, the rolling downs,
A childhood paradise to me.

Jenny Duckworth

Incident On Porthmeor Beach

Who
would
have
thought
that
the
poetry
of
the
sea
washing
away
a
line
of
nine
sand
pyramids
one
by
one
would
attract
the
imagination
of
so
many

Ralf Thorgood

THE BEAUTY OF LIFE

Aglaia. Whether a life of love or pain, beauty shines in a face,
For in a gentle nature, emotions show with charm and grace.
Years of tears and trials are hidden with perfect poise,
And patience to calm the sadness that this life employs.
To walk with grace a head held high, charming and refined,
So often shows in splendour of a face that's wise and kind.

Thalia. Humour is also a blessing that everyone commends,
Flourishing hearts with cheer, which laughter always ends.
A gift to render humour and a quip that brings acclaim,
From not a clown or jester, but fun that will not maim.
Would we all bloom with clever wit and easy flowing jollity,
Eloquence and the secret of fables would blossom in sweet poetry.

Euphrosyne. But, as mirth and happiness makes a face, blushing
pink and round,
Light-hearted smiles and merriment need not make a sound.
This, another form of beauty which shows in twinkling eyes,
Cascading the tears of laughter that end with contented sighs.
Take heart from those who gladden with just one special sound,
For this love flows and bursts with joy, then much gladness
will be found.

Concluding. For beauty lies in the eyes, showing grace,
humour and mirth,
Mirrored love in special ways which the good Lord desires on Earth.
He knew that men need strength to face life's worrying ways,
So He gave us special characters to chorus with His praise.
Enjoy a person's passions sometimes veiled in mystery,
Who show their warmth and charm as the 'Three Graces'
revealed sisterly.

Lucy-May Bloxham

Night Song

Sing! Golden bird,
Tempered in heaven's light!
Break, for a space
The dark grip of sleep.
Part, with your silvered cascades
Our tangled web of dreams.
Draw, for a moment,
A corner of night's curtain
And see ourselves
Play gods.
Catch, for an instant,
A flicker of action - there -
No, there! A shimmer of stardust
From an angel's heels
Before the curtain falls.

Jenny Hill

Wings Of Destiny

Softly, slowly, breezy blue
  blossom, heavy current through
floating, bouncing,
  walking hard
door locked shut, no escape
  darkness dwelling across a lake
mindless wonder
  wispy thoughts, time ticks slowly on a wall
sunset starts, time rolls on
  thoughts are changing must move on,
flying quick to reach the sun
  must not miss, just begun!

Emily Hayes

My Toy Boy

My toy boy
Is my joy boy
Means I'm singing all day long

My toy boy
Is my lifebuoy
Keeps me floating in life's pond

My toy boy
Is my playboy
Good enough for centre-fold

My toy boy
Is a schoolboy
Needs never to be told

My toy boy
Is a Fowey boy
Full of salty repartee

My toy boy
Is a choir boy
Well - it's just a fantasy

My toy boy
Is a didicoy
Loves bathing in the river

My toy boy
Is a paper boy
Who knows how to deliver

But thank the Lord
My toy boy
As a more than perfect lover
Has never muffed his lines
And tried to call me Mother.

June Lander

RAINDROPS DESCEND

Raindrops descend, puddles form,
A stream engulfed, a river is born,
A course is set, the sea to reach,
Meandering ponderously to a far off beach.

The sea reclaims its myriad young,
Kidnapped by clouds, thunder-slung;
The storm is long past with calm all around;
Albatross glide, with a whisper of sound.

Seagulls circle, dogfish sleep,
Gannets dive and dolphins leap,
But black clouds return and lightning flashes
O'er storm-tossed seas, as thunder crashes.

Once more a stealthy cloud abducts infant water,
The sea's own offspring: a son . . . a daughter;
The thief sets off at a windblown pace,
The anguished mother unable to chase.

The criminal finds refuge in a partisan crowd,
A formless body in a vaporous shroud;
The cloud has no guilt, shows no remorse,
But heads inland on a predestined course.

A hill stands guard, like a customs post;
It stabs the guilty, but allows past the host;
The rogue cloud is ruptured, severed seam and pleat,
Releasing its captives and accepting defeat.

Raindrops descend, puddles form,
A stream engulfed, a river is born,
A course is set, the sea to reach,
Meandering ponderously to a far off beach . . .

Clive Blake

Action Replay

I walked the dog.

Very reluctantly
I walked the dog.

It was raining
It was cold
But very reluctantly
I walked the dog.

The wind was howling
Around the corners of the house
I put his lead on
And took him out
It was raining
It was cold
But very reluctantly
I walked the dog.

I was tired
It was a late night last night
I was so tired
The lick of his tongue woke me up
I have no choice
He is so boisterous
He needs exercising
The wind was howling
Around the corners of the house
I put his lead on
And took him out
It was raining
But very, very reluctantly
I walked the dog.

Martin Spargo (12)

PEACE IN OUR TIME

It's a lovely sunny morning in the month of July,
a lone glider in the blue sky is circling high,
I get out the deckchair and fetch my paper,
cheeky kids at the back start another caper,
an Alsation started barking and goes on and on,
a woman shouts at her son, now what has he done?
A radio blasts out loudly disturbing the peace,
lawnmowers like Concorde, will the noise ever cease?
No peace for the weary so I'm soon on my way,
taking the dog for a walk down Pimbey Manor Bay,
along the old canal path and walk by the Severn,
far from the madding crowd, my idea of heaven,
I sit on the riverbank and spot a lone crane,
across the river a kingfisher dives again and again,
six splendid swans sail past to pastures new,
the dog takes a swim and a boat comes in view,
a lone rower passes by going a good steady pace,
a duck squawks noisily and leaves its nest place,
it's nice to relax here and get away from the din,
in the year 2000 it's a noisy world we live in.

Dennis Hughes

MY BIRTHDAY

I think my happiest day of the year
Has to be my birthday and all it holds dear
I don't bother to get up but wait you see
For someone to bring me a cup of tea.

The letter box rattles telling me the postman has been
I know somebody cares - it makes me feel like a queen
Cards from the family and friends I can see
How lucky I am - I'm so glad to be me.

A special one from my husband now married for 47 years
Words so special they sometimes reduce me to tears
Presents to open - and what do I see?
A bouquet of flowers have been delivered - just for me.

What more could I ask for - now I hope you can see
Why my birthday is the happiest day for me.

Marjorie Ridley

FISHERMEN

To look upon the silver sea
so calm, quiet and serene
only fishermen would know
how cruel and fierce it can be.

Only fishermen would be so brave
to sail alone upon that treacherous sea
to venture forth and ply their trade
with storms that rise within the hour.

To know beneath those forbidding waves
there lurks a force so strong
that mere man cannot do battle
with the winds and storm.

How hard they work, cold and wet
their hands so red and raw
but cheerfully they struggle on
to bring their catch back to the shore.

Exhausted and spent they sail their boats
back into port
to home and loved ones once more.

Lydia E Stanton

Walking Into Dream

Porlock feeling
Scaled the city
In a mist.
A dream rolled down the streets, and
Wound within the harbour;
Our place for clear thinking.

Sunless shadows, and swaying reflections
Lay lifeless on the surface of three weeks.
Lunar Park, lunar laughter, lunar beginnings -
We walked out of time, and
Missled with every drop of rain.
The flood of friendship
Flowed like a world in a wing-mirror;
Disappearing and prophetic.

I'll never let you go,
Even when summer drains through
The gutter grate.

An approach,
A knock, and
Ticking silence
Returned to the wall.
A trance of heaven
Broken by a messenger.
A stolen vision
Lanthanein in the harbour.

Edmund Garratt

A Quiet Hour

To sit alone for a quiet hour
Remembering, those days, now long past,
School days and those friends back then
Times that you thought, forever would last.

To reach back and name those girls and boys
Or should I leave them in peace and obscure?
No! These memories are ours, the joys of our youth,
Though years separate, forever, the memories endure.

To treasure the thoughts of things that we did
I wonder is it possible, could we meet and retell
Of those days and enjoy recalling the past,
Or has distance and time 'tolled the bell'.

Summer, the day was warm and school was out
Down to the swimming pool we would go,
Self learn to swim and dive, just us
No instructor or safety regulations to follow.

How we enjoyed those special hours,
In that pool that was filled by the tide,
And when the tides were at their neaps
Foul water rules, there were none to abide.

A member of the club, then change in the hut
If not around the corner, to put on swimming gear
How wonderful to recall, friends and the times we had
But for some of those friends, 'shed a tear'.

T W Denis Constance

END OF TERM

With sparkling eyes and voice too loud,
you join the small excited crowd.
Your school books stacked and locked away,
you've earned this longed-for holiday.

You learned your lessons, made the grade.
Prize-giving memories won't fade.
Next term you'll join a higher class,
new subjects and exams to pass.

But first, you have a holiday.
Time to relax and time to play.
You'll feel refreshed and full of hope
that with new lessons you will cope.

This life is but a term at school,
where we must learn each golden rule.
A set of lessons at each stage,
exams and then progress a grade.

New clothes next term; fresh, clean and bright.
They may be yellow, black or white.
Chosen with care to suit the term
bearing in mind what we must learn.

Each life a term, dull, boring, grey,
but followed by a holiday.
Our uniform, worn out with age
is tossed into an earthy grave.

Term ends. We die and friends are sad
when really they should be quite glad.
Happy to know we're on our way
to have a *super* holiday.

Raymond Black

A Question Of Childhood

Mummy? . . . Why does the world go round and round?

Mummy? . . . (Yes darling?) . . . Why is it that the sun comes out in the
day and the moon shines when it's dark,
And why does our Tabby miaow when little dogs bark?

Mummy? . . . (Y e s darling . . .) How do the clouds stay up in the sky
and who makes the wind that helps them to fly,
And why are some days hot and some days cool,
And Mummy? . . . (Yes darling . . .) Why does it always rain when
I'm home from school?

Mummy? . . . (Well darling, it's . . .) Why do some children walk
and others run as fast as they dare,
Whilst my friend William lives all day in a wheelchair,
Why doesn't he write to Jesus, a prayer or a little letter,
Do you think that *He* would make William very much better?

Mummy? . . . (Yes darling, I do, but . . .) Why do owls have such
big eyes,
And what happens in winter to the butterflies,
Do birds feel awfully cold in their nest,
And why does Aunty Silvia have such a big chest?

Mummy? . . . (Yes darling, owls have such big eyes because . . .) Why
was I born and from where did I come,
Was I the result of just having some fun,
Or was it intended that I should grow up with you and Dad,
To be loved and cared for and never feel sad,
To cuddle my teddy when going off to bed,
And fall asleep after the 'one more story' was read?

Mummy? . . . Why do some people kill other people?

R D Gruitt

Read, Spell Or Write

I can read but I'm dyslexic, it's spelling words that I find hard
Some consider me stupid and maybe a little retard
But I put my thoughts into poems so others might understand
That because I have problems with spelling inside there's
a capable man.

There are others like me all over the world who cannot read,
spell or write
Because we are thought of as backwards every day for our jobs
we must fight
It's an affliction we're born with, a condition we try to control
Understanding is all that we ask for that would put heart back
into our souls.

Try to be understanding if someone can't read, spell or write
And don't be so condescending, it could get you into a plight
Instead, don't be cruel be helpful for that would be good and nice
And if you could find time to help us, by giving some hope and advice.

So think on us, who can't read, spell or write, remember the
trouble we're in
It's only our memory refusing to take these important things in
None of us is perfect, our faults we must try to recall
For looking down upon others is the biggest fault of us all.

Keith Onslow

PARADISE LOST

What happened to that little cot,
that little cot of grey?
What happened to the garden
where once I used to play?

The golden pears, the walnut tree,
the plums of shiny blue;
What happened to the lawns of green
with their panoramic view?

And where's the cobbled path
with its borders neat and trim;
The rockery with its alpine blooms,
and graceful pines, so slim?

They've vanished, like the little gate,
the little gate of green
that let you into paradise,
that heaven so serene.

Now all I see is rubble, a pile, it's utter sin;
it's gone, that peaceful haven where once such joy reigned in.
Gone is the laughter, joy and mirth,
that precious place that saw my birth.

A Woolley

Eye To Eye

People are almost
Afraid these days,
To look you in the eye.
Such dreadful happenings.
Are we fearful
Of what we will see?

Don't be. Have courage.
Someone may give you
A message. And you, perhaps,
Send a ray of hope
Along the way for one sad soul
Who can hardly cope.

Cast off those shackles,
And you'll be free.
Yes, there is danger
Round every corner!
But never say die,
As my old Grandad
Used to say to me.

Mary Whitsitt

My Magic Box

I will place in my box

The crawl of a critter
The neck of a giraffe
The rotation of the earth

I will place in my box

The cry of a homeless child
The last autumn leaf to fall
The roar of the deep blue ocean

I will place in my box

A whisker from a purring cat
Fresh milk from the udders of a dairy cow
The whisper of true love

I will place in my box

The height of an eagle
The pride of a lion
The dress of a leopard.

Victoria Handley (10)

The Price Of Peace

P ut aside your anger
E vil thoughts of pain.
A ccept all forgiveness
C omrades again.
E xtend your hand

B etween north and south.
E xpress your feelings

W ith heart, soul and mouth,
I mpossible it's not
T hough each must believe, that
H urt is not the answer

Y our will, is to achieve.
O nly peace can be found
U nited and unarmed.

B egin to live,
Y et no longer harmed.

Becky Garbett (13)

The Long Wait

In early spring the snowdrops
Were a carpet of pure white
Then pink camellias and blue iris
Were a truly lovely sight.

You missed the mass of daffodils,
The roses came and went,
Gladiolas bloomed and faded,
'Fiery devils' blaze was spent.

Primroses, cowslips, lilac,
Clematis, white and blue,
Alyssum, lobelia,
To name just one or two.

Scarlet ranked geraniums,
Nasturtiums gold and flame,
The Russian sage, achillia,
But still you never came.

Heleniums and marigolds
Spread their goldenness,
But no! You didn't come till Christmas
And said 'The garden looks a mess.'

E A Groves

VINCENT VAN GOGH (1853 - 90)

Touched by empathy,
    and the fate of man,
a sunflower sought
    a worthy path.
Conveyed the music
    of the palette
colours flowed from inner light;
    released the spirit
of the flowers; heads still show
    a timeless life.
Brush strokes spread around
    like stitches
filled a landscape; framed a mood.
    Overtones beneath
the surface, reflect a darker
    point of view.
At heart the artist's
    infinite blackness
seldom he could paint away.
    A sunflower's love
of yellow brightness has left
    a brilliance to this day.

Josie May Hodges

DAYDREAMING OF HOME

Lying here thinking 'Where would I rather be?'
Stretched on a beach, being lapped by the sea,
Or maybe by a riverbank shaded by trees,
Smelling the grass and resting in peace
Standing tall on a hilltop, feeling the wind,
Getting up early to hear the birds sing,
Or the rain on my face as I walk a mile,
The happiness of children, that makes me smile.
Meeting with friends, chatting aloud,
Enjoying the laughter, hiding the cloud.
Deep down wondering 'Can time break the spell?'
Maybe I'll hear the words - that all is well
But when all's said and done, the best place for me,
Is at home, in my chair, with a good cup of tea!

Alice Turner

UNTITLED

Autumn.
Ochre yellows
Glossy greens
Mingle russets and browns
In autumn sheen.
Mixing shades
Like painters' palettes
Running into coloured streams
Of brilliant wonder -
Each colour strong in its desire
To mark the landscape
Before it rests to store the glory
Then downwards so gently it weeps
To form a blanket of winter sleep.

Carole Walters

How Dark Is The Night?

Dark, dark is the night
When, when will it be bright?
Time, time, how it drags
Time, time, how it lags

Night, night, how dark you are
But for a shining star
Night, night, how you creep around
Creeping, creeping, not a sound

Night, night, why didn't you go away?
Please, please don't stay
For how bleak and cold you are
The only light, a shining star

Susan Amphlett

April

The world has now come back into light
No longer winter's cold winds bite
The leaves uncurl upon the trees
And flutter in the gentle breeze.

Fresh showers help spring flowers grow
And once again there's lawns to mow
There's tulips painted pink and red
Now blanketing the flower bed.

Some hatched out birds take their first flight
Lambs race, and jump up in delight
Chestnut trees begin to flower
The sunshine has much greater power.

Wendy Dedicott

JUST ANOTHER DAY?

It's been
It's gone
The 20th century.

The new millennium
The parties were held
The fireworks went off
The 21st century.

What of the future
Will it all change?
Of course it will
But just as the moment
It's difficult to know
What to expect - tomorrow.

Mary A Slater

MEMORY

Relentlessly the tide of life moves on,
Each rolling wave enveloping the last,
Its swirling waters flooding all that's gone,
Determined to obliterate the past.

But memory defeats the ruthless surge
And keeps alive departed joy and pain,
Engendering a strange pathetic urge
To live our past experiences again.

To man alone belong these precious powers
To conjure back past laughter and past tears,
Restraining greedy time ere he devours
The magic moments of our vanished years.

Evelyn Scott Brown

ATTICS

Under the roof top
in a cemetery of powder dust
assorted objects
are sprawled
still, silent, sleeping
in the darkness.
Unused, unvalued, unloved.
Yet not completely discarded
as they lie patiently
like mute mummies in a tomb,
suspended in time,
awaiting the daylight
of their re-awakening.

What broken dreams
and buried wounds
slumber
in the secret chamber
of our minds,
stored away
out of sight
not to plague or torture
with the pain of a delight
or the delight of a pain,
lost beyond our recall,
dormant, festering,
they tremble and twitch
for the dawning
of their release.

Helen Dalgleish

My Bike

I had a trike
  Not a bike
When I was small.
  Then I grew tall
And had a bike
  Not a trike

The bike I had was old
  To me it was like gold.
It took me far and near
  In the same gear
And lasted many a year

But going down a hill
  I had a spill
This broke my bike in two
  There was nothing I could do
So I am telling you

I Millington

To Paul and Rachelle Hornby

(Of a marriage made in heaven. 21st February 2000)

We dream of things sometimes too beautiful to say
The valleys so deep, to the echoes of the wind that blows
A sideway to our hearts.
To the cry of a lonesome wolf.
Of the deepest forests, to the snow-covered mountains.
And of the river that cries so sweet to the moon above of starry bright.
In the midnight hour never alone, this timeless love will never die.
The twilight hour soon be near as two hearts beat forever more.
Hand in hand we walk together along the silk sand shores
Of ever-lasting love, with the cool ocean blue as white horses
Ride to footprints we leave behind.
The vows we speak we stand together, eye to eye we see each other
Of the love we have, more greater than that of the words we speak.
Timeless times we spend together to the end we do spend
Till God's blue heaven.

Craig Alan Hornby